The Practice of Supervision in Social Work

A Guide for Staff Supervisors

Ilse J. Westheimer

Ward Lock Educational

To the memory of my Mother who cared so much

ISBN 0 7062 3644 0

© Ilse Westheimer 1977. All rights reserved. No part of this publication may be reproduced, stored in a retrieval system or transmitted, in any form or by any means, electronic, mechanical, photocopying, recording or otherwise, without the prior permission of the copyright owner.
First published 1977

Set in 11 on 12 point Plantin
by Computacomp (UK) Limited, Fort William
and printed by Robert MacLehose and Company Limited
for Ward Lock Educational
116 Baker Street, London W1M 2BB
A member of the Pentos Group
Made in Great Britain

Contents

Acknowledgments		v
Preface		vii
Foreword by Margaret Eden OBE		ix

1 The Social Services Department
Introduction	1
The outcome of reorganization	2
The need to support social workers	4
The effect of the tier structure	6
Practice of the social worker	7
Summary	12

2 The functions of a supervisor
Historical development of social work training	13
The position of the supervisor in departmental structure	15
Management elements in supervision	16
The teaching element in supervision	17
The meaning of support in supervision	19
Encouraging objectivity	21

3 The skills of the supervisor
The need for a change in attitude to supervision	25
Conditions required for sound supervision	26
The capacity and skills of the supervisor	27

4 Some practical issues for new supervisors
Guidelines for a beginning supervisor and a newly qualified worker	38
Restricted worker capacity: problems for the supervisor	43

5 Factors in learning and teaching
Adults as learners	49
Early learning climate	50

The ambivalent element in learning	52
Personality functioning in learning	53
Climate for learning	57
Common stages in learning	62
Individual learning patterns	70
Motivation, capacity and opportunity	72

6 The practicality of caseload and workload management

Rationing	78
The supervisor's task in relation to caseload management	81
A method of caseload/workload management *Dorothy Lloyd-Owen*	81
Introducing caseload management into the agency *Joan Hodgets*	90
A look at three workloads *Susan Smith*	98

7 First assessment of the level of social work functioning 106

Model A: Assessment of a newly qualified worker	112
Model B: Assessment of a social work assistant	114
Model C: An alternative approach to assessing a worker	118
Model D: Assessment of an unqualified worker	126

8 Evaluation

The nature of evaluation	138
Evaluation is a judgment based on evidence	140
Towards a common minimal standard	141
Areas for evaluation	155

9 Consultation

What is consultation?	157
The consultant's equipment	162

References	166
Bibliography	168
Index	171

Acknowledgments

Intuitive understanding that learning goes on throughout life occurred relatively early with me and is linked in my memory to an inscription by my infant school teacher, Betty Schleifer, who wrote:

Schau in die Welt mit wachen Sinnen
Wirst immer Neues ihr abgewinnen.*

Teaching and learning are interlinked activities; the teaching of supervision has always meant for me learning more about the practice of supervision. Hence I wish to thank first and foremost all those senior and principal social workers who have contributed to a more thorough understanding of the nature of social work supervision by means of their participation in the various courses and seminars for which I have been responsible in different parts of the country. I want to express my special thanks to all those staff supervisors of the Berkshire Social Services Department, with whom I have been privileged to work for the past four years and whose encouragement and contributions have been most welcome. Specific work of the early seminar groups is included in chapter 6. Special thanks go to Joan Smethurst for her individual contribution.

I particularly want to thank the contributors to the chapter on caseload and workload management, Dorothy Lloyd-Owen, Joan Hodgets and Susan Smith. The practical application and methods described in this chapter form an essential part of social work supervision and this publication would be incomplete without it. I am especially indebted to Dorothy Lloyd-Owen who gave so readily of her time and maintained enthusiasm throughout. I am indebted to Anne Vickery for her major contribution towards the conceptionalization of caseload management.

My thanks are due also to Mary Hellier for reading and criticising the total manuscript, to Margaret Eden, formerly Head Social Worker, Bethlem Royal and Maudsley Hospital, for reading portions of the manuscript and for her helpful suggestions.

*Translation: 'Look into the world with open eyes and you will continuously see and learn anew.'

I am grateful to all those social work teachers who taught by personal example and at different stages of my professional development, that the learning of social work requires as well as good teaching, caring and support. I wish to thank particularly Isabel Miller, my first tutor in social work; Margaret Eden, my first supervisor in the mental health field and Elizabeth Horder, my former senior colleague who was then Head Social Worker at the Child Guidance Training Centre.

I also wish to thank the late Professor Gordon-Hamilton for her inspiration, positive criticism and support.

Finally, I want to extend my thanks to those social work teachers whose writings have had a profound influence on my own supervisory and teaching practice, in particular Virginia Robinson, Charlotte Towle and most of all Bertha Reynolds whose clear thinking and wisdom I have found indispensable.

Preface

This book was written in response to requests from senior social workers and staff supervisors in various parts of the country, who expressed the need to have beside them some concrete material giving direction and guidance on the functions of social work supervisors. This request was also invariably made at the completion of every short course on supervision for which I was responsible, when staff supervisors pressed for written material that would sustain them in their task and underpin their new learning.

To provide such an aid seems especially important as it appears that the majority of staff supervisors are receiving little or no help from their departments; many are thrown in at the deep end to sink or swim and survive as best they can.

I have been aware for a considerable period of time that here in Britain we lack opportunities to learn how to practise the kind of staff supervision that enables social workers to develop greater competence and higher standards of work. It was this recognition that activated my interest in setting up, with colleagues, the first staff supervision option as part of the courses in further social work studies at the National Institute in Social Work Training in 1969, and later to accept an appointment with the Berkshire Social Services where work in the field of supervision was to be the primary task.

The writing of this book was more difficult than I had envisaged. Choices had to be made as to what should be included and what had to be omitted. These decisions are much easier to make in active teaching when the feed-back from the group helps to determine to some extent both the content and the pace. I hope that I have made the appropriate choices. The reader will here be the judge.

I was initially puzzled about the difficulty I experienced in writing the chapter on the Social Services. Only when I started to think and reflect on the nature of the task of the social worker, did I become aware of the extent of my anger about the many conflicting demands made on young social workers only recently qualified, who carry such a heavy load in the present structure and often without the necessary support. This general comment is related to the knowledge I have gained of the functioning of many social services departments in different parts of the country through the teaching of staff supervision. To my knowledge there are few, if any, social services departments who have stressed, as has the Berkshire Social Services Department, the importance of good supervision practice, and who have actually provided ongoing learning opportunities for staff supervisors in seminar groups and in individual consultations.

I also want to make it explicit that illustrations and examples cited throughout the book come from very many different sources.

The aim of this book is to encourage staff supervisors* to think through their functions and tasks, to offer some theoretical knowledge about the adult learner, to give guidelines for use in practice and to test out how the principles of supervision operate in our present organizations. It is my hope that this small book will assist supervisors in carrying out the important task of supervision in a disciplined, systematic and objective manner, yet will stimulate reflective thinking leading to the development of individual styles and ways of working.

I feel privileged to be able to work so closely with the various groups of staff supervisors and through these seminar sessions to have the opportunity of continuing my own learning.

Ilse J. Westheimer

---

*The term 'supervisor' is used for anyone who has the function of supervising staff whether as a team leader or as a senior social worker. The focus in this publication is on function not on tier.

Foreword *Margaret Eden,* OBE

The subject of this book, staff supervision, is vital to a profession concerned with the quality of its practice and its author is a person eminently fitted to write about it. Ilse Westheimer writes out of many years' experience as a supervisor of students, as a teacher of staff supervisors and as a consultant in a social services department. The Association of Psychiatric Social Workers, of which she was a member, was a group small enough to give personal support to its members and one of its main concerns in the 1950s and 1960s was the improvement of standards of supervision both for students and for junior staff. Indeed, the first papers published in this country on supervision were written by psychiatric social workers.

Ilse Westheimer feels deeply about the plight of young social workers in large, complex departments and that of their often inexperienced supervisors. She stresses the necessity for newly qualified workers to have the tuition and nurture in their early years which can enable them to develop the strength and expertise to stand up to the strains and demands that are inherent in their work. The patterns of care and relationships in the agency are reflected in their behaviour and attitudes with clients and other workers.

Ilse Westheimer's views on the value of supervision are supported by proposals of the British Association of Social Workers which are at present before the membership on the subject of accreditation in social work: 'A period of carefully supervised practice with a realistic workload is called for, if a newly qualified social worker is to be able to use and consolidate his training, and to develop into a competent self-regulating practitioner.'

The book encourages social workers to ensure that recognition is given to supervision. It provides a detailed analysis of the tasks of supervisors and offers methods of fulfilling them. I trust that this book will be studied by all concerned with staff supervision.

1 The social services department

Introduction
The capacity of staff supervisors to influence the standard of practice achieved by social workers is at the heart of this book. Since most supervisors operate within social services departments we must begin by examining those structural factors in the new organization which impinge on the social worker's function. The supervisor must weigh up the prevailing conditions in the department and assess how these help or hinder the development of essential social work skill. The size, the structure and the policy of an organization have an immense impact on social workers; in turn, their performance affects intimately all clients who call on the department for help.

The reorganization of the local authority's social services in 1971 has brought about vast changes in the structure of the organization and in the pattern of social work practice. The amalgamation of the three original departments, Health, Welfare and Children, into one large comprehensive department called for changes in orientation and commitment and required an extension of functions. Social workers had to rethink their *raison d'être*, come to terms with the new responsibilities, extend their work into unfamiliar areas, deal with feelings of loss of identity and recreate for themselves a new sense of belonging. During the initial phase of reorganization when too much change occurred in too short a period, lack of a clear purpose brought upheaval and disorientation to the department as a whole and separately to individual members of staff. Subsequent changes over a prolonged period caused further personal insecurity and stress. These events have had a profound effect on the functioning of the social worker and on the kind and quality of help available to clients.

Now, four years later, it can be seen that the comprehensive department is better placed than were the separate departments to take an overall view of existing community needs and to avoid duplication of services. The new department has more resources than any one department had in the past and a broader range of staff, occupational therapists, home helps, play group leaders, day centre and residential staff, and can therefore offer a greater variety of services to clients.

Before it had a chance to establish itself, however, new legislation added further responsibilities to the department's already heavy load. It could not but fall short of widely held expectations. The question of appropriate resources to implement new legislation does not appear to have troubled ambitious politicians. Now tasks have become almost infinite, boundaries hardly seem to exist and social service departments are expected to be all things to all men at all times. For example, during periods of industrial action when the essential supply services are affected (electricity, gas, etc.), social workers have to give priority to resulting hardship at the expense of ongoing work with regular clients who need a steady relationship. Erratic contacts, when clients are picked up one day only to be dropped the next, are unhelpful. While the comprehensive department is better placed to detect needs and problems in the community, it cannot meet all needs without an increase in resources.

The outcome of reorganization

In general, economic and practical needs are given priority over emotional and psychological needs. Crises take precedence over preventative work. For example, marital disharmony receives little attention until there is a complete breakdown and the children have to be taken into care, or the acute depression of one partner necessitates admission to a mental hospital. Sustained and extended work with a depressed mother, though she may be the mainstay of the family, is rare, even though insufficient help at the crucial time will more than double the department's work in the end. The cost in terms of human stress and strain cannot be calculated. The aim of the reorganized social services department to prevent social distress, as embodied in the Seebohm Report (1968) paras. 427–30, is a long way from realization.

Hence the social work profession together with the social services departments need to take stock of present trends and alter course.

The generally held assumption that the department's broad brief can be adequately carried out despite present restraints on resources, must be clarified and challenged. Questions have to be faced about the priorities of need. In the past, when there were separate departments each with a system of defined eligibility, this was a simpler task. Classifying people in relation to their needs and problems established guidelines as to who was eligible for help. Those who did not fit into the criteria of one department might well fit into that of another and could be re-referred. The position today is very different. There is now only one door of entry to the local authority's social services; this calls for understanding and rigorous examination of resources. Many departments retreat from a task that poses complex questions such as Whom does one help? Whose need is greater?

Which handicaps take priority? How can the the needs of the low-income family whose physical health is undermined be equated against the needs of a family whose faulty relationship pattern is affecting the emotional health of the children? How does one balance the physical and emotional needs of a young child with those of an elderly woman in her last few years of life?

These are complex and difficult questions that have in the main been left unanswered. In the absence of a declared policy on priorities the client service is likely to be uneven and at times unfair. A heavy burden is also placed on the intake social worker when he is expected to reach decisions that the department as a whole has failed to make. In this situation individual social workers have to fall back on personal judgement based on their own perception, understanding, skills, experiences and values, and at times on moods of the moment. There is a danger that social workers, already burdened by a heavy workload opt for hasty decisions, and act on prevailing feelings rather than on a comprehensive diagnostic assessment. It is the responsibility of the department to ensure that decisions are taken for objective reasons and not because social workers are under pressure. R.A. Parker (1967) suggests that where demand for help exceeds supply and extra resources are not forthcoming, 'the demand for a service normally needs to be restrained or its nature and quality modified.' He considers ways in which the problems of scarcity have been dealt with in the past and demonstrates the likely results when an organization does not use a defined system of eligibility.

Dilution of service is one possible consequence when everybody gets something but only a few are helped effectively. Social Services departments are familiar with this way of operating. Deterrents are another means to stem the flow of requests. The poor reputation of the service can act as a deterrent to potential clients, as can poor premises, cold unfriendly waiting rooms, casual reception and rushed interviews. All these have the effect of subtly keeping the volume of work within more manageable bounds. Some deterrents are used more consciously than others. Parker also comments on the delaying tactics, so relevant today and quoted here for this reason:

> Delay may also become a deterrent; two hours sitting in an outpatients department is a cost which once experienced may deter except in serious circumstances. Waiting lists may also shrink as a result of what is now respectably termed spontaneous remission. Time spent on the list may appear to be a therapy in itself.

R.A. Parker gives an extract from John Stroud's *The Shorn Lamb*:

> About a week later I (a child care officer) was passing a dark grocer's shop in the High Road when out came a fat, sad looking woman, Miss Niff, the social worker from the Clinic. When she saw me she hailed me with a mournful hoot. 'Hilloo, Hilloo! I vos going to tiliphone you!'
> 'Oh, yes?'
> 'Our leedle friend Egbert,' she said, falling into step beside me and nodding her head sagaciously.
> 'Yiss, vell, ve haf seen through him!'
> 'Oh, have you?' I said disappointed. I'd known him for a couple of years and I could not see through him. I felt ashamed and chagrined that Miss Niff could do better than I could.
> 'Ho, yiss,' she said, still nodding, 'Hev no fears, shall I tell you vot ve propose to do? Ve are going to put Egbert on the vaiting list.'
> 'My word!' I said, adding cautiously: 'Is that good?'
> 'Ho, very good,' she said. 'Very effective, it is a method of treatment with a very high success rate: ve put them on the list and by the time they are actually seen at the Clinic nearly ninety percent are cured.'

At least little Egbert and his mum knew that he was *only* on the waiting list. The position is infinitely worse when clients are given to understand that they will be seen next week, but next week never comes.

The need to support social workers

The clientele of the social worker is comprised of people who are overwhelmed by social, economic, or personal difficulties, and who are expressing these difficulties in a variety of ways. An organization that has as its primary aim helping people in need, must build into its structure a support system that sustains the workers in this task. This, unfortunately, is not always found in the social services departments, and leads social workers to complain that pressures on them frequently tend to be disregarded. In the absence of a support system that takes account of the strain and pressures arising from the very nature of the work, individual social workers may become preoccupied with their own problems and like their clients, feel helpless and overwhelmed. This diminishes their ability to help their clients and lowers the department's standard of service.

There are two misconceptions in management: one is that 'mature' people can operate independently under any conditions at all times; the other arises from a lack of appreciation of the anxiety-producing nature of the work and the consequent feeling of depletion. Social workers who support people in the community, themselves need support if they are to fulfil their tasks adequately. Workers who feel themselves depleted are not able to meet their clients' needs. People who are not cared for cannot extend genuine care to others. Care and support should begin at the top of an organization and pervade the whole atmosphere of a large establishment. It can be demonstrated through providing adequate secretarial assistance, suitable interviewing rooms, manageable workloads with some leeway in time arrangements, opportunities for sharing in discussions and being consulted when appropriate; all these are important factors in reducing work tension and anxiety. Staff supervision is an essential part of this support.

Effective communication throughout the department is another vital link in the support system. When matters of importance are not communicated, staff can experience this as being overlooked, excluded and as being thought of little consequence. It encourages staff to split the organization into 'them' and 'us' in a way that is detrimental to their work.

The mode of communication has to be adapted to the size of the organization. In a small department, discussion can be face to face. This is clearly not possible in a large organization. Also, some decisions have to be taken quickly and do not allow for appropriate consultations. Many communications will have to be made in writing to ensure that information is disseminated. Written comments and statements however can appear to lend finality to a subject matter where this was not the intention of the writer. Memoranda can act as irritants if their purpose is obscure or the wording makes for mystification. Management of a large organization need to take special care to counteract the effect of size, and to find means by which to demonstrate that the individual worker is important.

Poor communication also occurs when information is given but not heeded. This can happen when the recipient guards against hearing those messages that make him feel uncomfortable, inadequate and threatened. It occurs especially when a number of staff have stepped into new roles, are carrying fresh responsibilities, have had inadequate preparation for new tasks which nevertheless have to be tackled. This has been the case in the social services and has affected the functioning of the social worker as it has that of the director. When people are uncertain of their own competence, communication is impoverished because of their fear of revealing too much of themselves. This furthers the tendency to withhold, the reluctance to share, and reinforces the need to appear to be in control. When staff are preoccupied with functioning in their own new roles, little energy is left over to support colleagues. These factors greatly affect the task of the supervisor.

The effect of the tier structure
With the growth in social services departments there has been an increase also in the 'strata' or 'tier' pattern. Authorities have devised various hierarchies. With the second reorganization in 1974 some increased the steepness of the hierarchy by adding still further tiers. The rationale for this was far from clear and is reflected in the number of appointments that were made at that time with explicit rank but without a specified job description. At this early stage some experimentation is useful since the optimum shape of a hierarchy in the social services has yet to be worked out. Care must be taken to minimize organizational splitting which is encouraged by the tier structure and to ensure that senior staff do not become too remote from the function of the department.

In many professions the practitioner is seen as the most important member since he supplies the service to the client. He is the foundation stone of the organization. If the foundation is firm the structure has every prospect of being steady and effective. Without competent practitioners the service to clients will be inadequate however sophisticated the skills of the managers. The present structure has conferred much higher status and salary to the managers of the department than to the practising social workers. This has done nothing to enhance social work practice, but instead has diminished the importance of the social work practitioner whose place is commonly perceived to be at the bottom of the pyramid.

It is interesting to speculate how this topsy turvey situation has come about and to fathom the reasons that prevented a social work profession from initial strong comment on the obvious consequences of such a structure, instead of giving implicit sanction.

Whatever happened in the early 1970s, it is now urgent to consider the steps that need to be taken to put the value back into social work and to give explicit recognition to skilled social work practice; if this is not done soon social work practice will show a prolonged downward trend. The rigid separation of management roles from social work tasks, now common in many departments, where principal social workers and sometimes even senior social workers are discouraged from having even a small caseload, this 'never the twain shall meet' attitude, has contributed to the devaluing of social work practice, to organizational splitting and to the diminishing quality in the service to clients. It is not surprising therefore that social work practice is viewed by some as only a stepping stone to higher spheres. The committed social work practitioner gets little encouragement in the present climate. He is frequently viewed as lacking in drive and ambition because he channels his energies into increasing his skills as a social worker. These circumstances have contributed to the present situation where there are all too few experienced social workers; the majority of clients are helped by recently qualified or by unqualified social workers. The proposal of the Seebohm Report for a 'career structure' requires urgent implementation. The Report states: 'The career structure of the social services department should allow a proportion of posts for highly skilled practitioners to advance in salary and status, without necessarily assuming substantial administrative responsibilities, though they would of course be expected to undertake some supervision and consultancy work.' A few departments have now made a start in establishing a limited career structure for practitioners; but this does not yet go far enough either in terms of recognition, advancement or further training facilities.

The Seebohm Committee's insistence (Seebohm Report, 1968, paras. 526, 516) 'that the family or individual should be the concern of *one* social worker with a comprehensive approach to the social problems of his clients' has shifted the balance too far away from specific knowledge, skills and understanding and the previous specialisms.

While many social workers will be in sympathy with the Report and also with the view expressed by Ruskin a long time ago, quoted by Titmus (1968), 'not only is there but one way of doing things rightly, but there is only one way of seeing them and that is seeing the whole of them', many are now also questioning its practicality. It is important to *see* the whole range of community needs, to see the total needs of a family, to see all the factors in a client's situation. It is equally essential, however, to recognize individual social work competence and limitations. Emphasis on the all-purpose social worker should not serve as a camouflage for mediocre work.

Are the huge demands on the social worker bearable and manageable? How does this effect the quality of social work? How can the scarce human resources be used to the best advantage of clients? These questions face all social workers; the supervisor faces them continuously when dealing with allocation of work. The service of the department depends to a very large extent on the skills of the social workers and how their individual qualities are put to use. Many promising workers have moved from social work practice to the management of social work; others have moved into the realm of teaching where more satisfactory work conditions prevail; others still have moved into settings that are seen to put a higher value on the quality of social work performance and are providing a calmer climate in which to practise. As experienced social workers have been drawn away from practice in the social services the important task of helping clients largely remains with recently qualified staff.

Practice of the social worker

What, then, is the equipment of the recently qualified social worker; the worker now most frequently in contact with clients? Beginning knowledge and skill are acquired during training and serve as a foundation for future development in the job. Hence, what is taught, how and when it is taught, are factors of importance. Teaching establishments in social work vary and, like the social services departments, depend on the quality of their staff. Learning in social work is based on the integration of theory and practice.

The 'generic' concept in social work education, for many years a feature in American social work, has now, many years later, been accepted in this country. Hence there is now recognition that all social work education rests on common basic knowledge such as the understanding of social factors and of dynamic psychology, and these subjects form part of the curriculum. The term 'generic' in no way suggests, as sometimes implied, that social work training can prepare social workers to do everything anywhere somehow! The misuse of the term 'generic' in this country has contributed to the present confusion concerning its use in social work. Gordon Hamilton's (1951) definition is very clear. 'Generic', she states, 'does not mean "elementary", but rather the basic knowledge of social factors and dynamic psychology for effective operation in any setting, calling for the same essential skills.' Her emphasis on the common knowledge base in no way suggests that specific knowledge is not equally essential. A. Vickery in *Social Work Today* Vol. 4 no. 9, also makes this explicit by the practical examples offered. She suggests that the concept of 'generic' as used in Britain is probably only valid at a fairly high level of abstraction.

> For example, it can be said that people suffering from the effects of 'separation' experience many similar feelings and difficulties and that an understanding of, and an ability to deal with the effects of separation are things all social workers need to have. This is undoubtedly true. But social work practice does not rest at that level of abstraction. Separation occurs for a particular individual in a particular social situation, and is presented to a particular social worker in a particular organization. The situation and needs of Mary Jane aged six, taken into care because of the inability of her mother to cope with her husband's imprisonment, are surely vastly different from the situation and needs of either Mary Jane's mother or of her father. If one considers the concept of 'institutionalization', it might be agreed that at that level of abstraction Mary Jane and her father have much in common – Mary Jane in her community home, and her father in prison. But the social worker who is perhaps very knowledgeable about intervention with staff on behalf of children in a children's home, does not by virtue of that knowledge have the ability to intervene as effectively with staff in a prison.

In the present climate of change many social work courses have experimented with teaching various social work methods. Some have extended the curriculum to include theoretical knowledge of different methods of intervention, others have aimed at providing also practice opportunities. Experimentation in general is to be welcomed. It is necessary for the growth of a profession, provided that the experimenters are open minded and have the moral courage to declare when it does not work out for the recipient. Social work teachers have been reticent to admit that there is lack of knowledge and practice in hitherto neglected methods, such as group work; they have not drawn enough attention to the difficulty of learning and consolidating a number of social work methods in a limited time. Like their colleagues in the social services they have allowed themselves to be swept along by public demand. The social work educator should know that while much can be taught only some of it can be absorbed and still less can be applied.

The key to successful teaching lies in presenting the right amount of material at the right time. Too much knowledge spread over too wide a field usually leads to bewilderment and difficulty in application. These considerations are of course relevant to field work learning; when the student is plunged continually into unfamiliar areas, great uncertainty is created which precludes him from building up slowly some expertise in a small area of work. As a result anxiety mounts and learning capacity is lowered. Without specific knowledge of the nature, onset, causation and duration of the problem, without knowing something about the possible approaches towards solutions, the student (and later the worker) will continue to fumble in the dark, at great cost to himself and his clients. It is important to provide opportunities that enable the learner to extend the understanding derived from one case to others, thus to build up an organized body of knowledge as the basis of effective practice. Knowledge increases security and lessens anxiety; especially when this knowledge can be underpinned by insights derived from practice.

In general, recently qualified social workers have a broader view of society and are better acquainted with certain behavioural sciences than their predecessors. They have had the opportunity to learn about the different methods of intervention and their uses; at the same time, fewer opportunities are now available to work with a limited range of clients over a period of time. Because of this, the chances of building up expertise in any one area is reduced and consolidation of knowledge and skill is slowed down.

Senior staff should know what level of professional development to expect of a newly qualified social worker and make only realistic demands. The Seebohm Report (1968) suggests that 'on first entry to the service, the range of work of the newly qualified social worker would normally be limited.' Exceptionally, some supervisors have been successful in selecting for newly qualified staff a limited caseload in range and size.

The management of the wide range of cases of the all purpose social worker is of great concern to many, not least to the social worker himself and the supervisor. The assumption that social workers can adequately deal with the complexity of human problems from cradle to grave, from the physically sick to the mentally ill, is unrealistic.

Social workers work with people who cannot cope with some aspect of their lives, who feel alone, unhappy and bereft. To work with people in stressful situations and to be of help when everyone feels helpless, requires a degree of certainty about professional competence. This derives largely from theoretical and practical knowledge of the problem subject matter in all its dimensions. R.A. Titmus (1968) has put it in this way: 'They (professional people) want to be more certain about themselves and their identity in an increasingly complex society. To acquire and cultivate one small allotment of skill and knowledge where one feels somewhat more secure in the vastness of the knowable is a great comfort.' Social services departments must see that such opportunities are provided. The social worker requires this degree of security to be able to feel that he has indeed something to contribute to the helping process and he therefore needs specific knowledge and skill. For example, when a small child is about to be separated from his mother, the social worker does not deal with separation per se but with the personal experience of this particular child and his mother. (See Heinicke and Westheimer, 1965; Westheimer 1970).

To be able to do this, a wide range of knowledge specific to separation is required, a thorough understanding of the complex feelings inherent in these situations. Such knowledge is essential to the understanding of this particular child and his idiosyncratic responses. Knowledge of developmental stages as related to separation is equally important, as is the understanding of this child's tie with his mother and the effect of this on the kind of relationships he will be likely to establish in the new setting. This, of course, is also dependent on what the setting has to offer, for example the capacity of the nursery staff to establish substitute rather than fragmented care. The social worker must also be familiar with the different phases of separation and have the skill to help staff to understand the meaning of the child's behaviour at a particular stage of separation. On the other hand, the social worker requires knowledge also of the maternal feelings, reponses and behaviour surrounding separation, and skill in keeping alive the feelings for the absent child, and so to increase the possibility of a speedy and less painful reunion of mother and child.

The development of such specific bodies of knowledge and skill is absolutely essential to good social work practice. Social services departments need to give urgent and serious consideration to how this can be achieved, how to build in opportunities for acquiring these skills. The answer is certainly not to be found in sending people on more and more short courses. Some shift of orientation in thinking as well as in organizing is required. As matters stand, most social workers carry not only a large caseload but one with a wide range of clients and problems. There is not enough opportunity for social workers to deepen their knowledge and skill. When time is short and opportunities for comparing cases are small, social workers have less chance to consolidate their knowledge. They are increasingly voicing dissatisfaction with the present pattern of work; they are troubled and made very anxious by unrealistic assumptions of being able to work equally well with all manner of clients, and having to deal with different client crises at any time without adequate preparation. As put by one worker: 'it is the mix of crisis I cannot cope with any longer.' (She has since left social work altogether!) This situation is not necessarily helped by the worker's awareness of his own limitation and lack of knowledge.

In practical terms this can mean that one social worker in a brief span of time may have to deal with an emergency admission of a woman to a mental hospital, with a case of potential battering, and with the predicament of a family where the wife and mother is suffering from multiple sclerosis. How is the newly qualified social worker to acquire adequate knowledge to deal in a competent way with these different but very demanding cases? What can be done for more experienced social workers to provide the opportunities for improving the quality of their work instead of increasing the volume of work? These are questions that must exercise the staff supervisor in particular.

The Seebohm Report's message, that social workers should undertake a 'wider range of social work functions' has been widely interpreted to mean that social workers will carry out all social work functions. Hence the tendency is to stress the similarity in individual workers' contributions while minimizing their differences. Individual aptitudes and skills often remain unrecognized or undeclared, yet a team's richness depends on these and the way in which they complement each other. These differences will bring about challenging questioning necessary to a dynamic team whose members continue to learn. It is not suggested that supervisors fail to recognize the different interests and contributions of team members but rather that there is a reluctance to give explicit recognition and encouragement to these.

Surely social workers must discourage the image of being 'Jack of all Trades' even though initially this may have a desired omnipotent ring; but the 'master of none' aspect, the coping by just holding the head above water adds great strain to the social worker's already demanding task. The attempt to cope with everything usually results in the end with not coping well with anything; just as the attempt to be available to everybody mainly results in not being effectively available to anybody.

Summary

Four years after the establishment of the comprehensive social services departments it is timely to consider where we have arrived and in what direction now to proceed. How well has the brief been fulfilled? Are there adequate learning opportunities for social workers so that they can improve the quality of service to clients? What changes in the conception and organization of the departments would raise the standard of practice? How can the social worker's tasks be made more manageable, and in what way can better use be made of scarce human resources? Taking an overall view of the present scene, it seems that the net has been cast too wide and needs pulling in. Social services departments are not in a position to deal with all crisis situations in society; attempts to do so make for dilution of services and only minimal help to clients. The actual capacity of the department needs to be declared and understood by social services committees and the wider community (including the potential clientele). They should know what services are available in their area and what are the gaps.

A more rational system of priorities in relation to client need is required although the difficulties in establishing it are acknowledged. The broad brief and diffuse function of social workers heightens the problem of priority. The allocation of time and skill to existing and new clients, as between crisis and prevention, pose complex questions for the supervisor. Some means of managing caseloads are explored in Chapter 6.

The many functions and responsibilities of the social worker require urgent review. When human resources are scattered over too wide a field, wastage of potential social work skill occurs. This is due to two factors inherent in the situation; the slow pace at which consolidation of knowledge and skill can take place, and the social workers' expenditure of energy in worrying about his capacity to tackle the task; this energy would otherwise be directly available in work with clients.

The aim here is not to make detailed recommendations, but rather to bring to the fore questions and reservations already in the mind of many social workers; to stimulate and encourage all staff supervisors, whether team leaders or senior social workers, to play an important part in appraising and reassessing the present situation; to encourage participation in planning which will improve client service and increase job satisfaction for the practitioner.

2 The functions of a supervisor

Staff supervision in the local authority social services exists to ensure that clients are given the best possible service and that the work of the department is carried out evenly and effectively. Supervisors are concerned with the availability of resources, human and material, and should ensure that these are used to the best advantage, whilst deficiencies are declared. The staff supervisor (for the sake of clarity the supervisor is referred to throughout as she, the social worker as he) should also monitor and aim to raise social work standards, in both the quality and quantity of work undertaken. It is the supervisor who carries ultimate responsibility for allocating appropriate cases to individual social workers and ensures that the team of social workers are making realistic decisions about scarce resources of skill and time. This requires clarity of vision and firmness of purpose. The supervisor must appraise the total scene, i.e. the team's commitment and output, yet also be capable of paying attention to detail such as one area of a worker's performance or one client's functioning. It is not always appreciated that this requires special knowledge and skill.

Historical development of social work training

By the nineteenth century a number of voluntary agencies had come into being whose aim was to meet social need whilst also trying to understand its causes. The early settlement movement and the Charity Organization Society (COS) were in the forefront of this development, and it was mainly due to their initiative that a form of systematic training was begun in Britain and in the USA.

The earliest students were small groups of voluntary workers who gathered around some experienced leaders, like Octavia Hill, whose creative imagination, enthusiasm and devotion to the task of social betterment inspired in them a similar desire to help the poor. In 1873 Octavia Hill described her training objectives (Bell, 1942):

> Fundamentally the training for all these workers was the same: they must all learn to deal with people, to understand the conditions

under which they lived and the ways in which these could be improved: they must be familiar with the various agencies for helping people.

Around 1890 a joint training for settlement work and rent collecting was set up at the Women's University Settlement in London and in 1896 the National Union of Women Workers and the staff of the COS combined to form a Joint Lectures Committee. (Content of lectures contained in *Twenty-eighth Annual COS Report 1897*). This body set up an eighteen months' training scheme consisting of lectures and concurrent fieldwork placements for voluntary and paid workers. At that time similar developments were also afoot in New York. The COS started a course of lectures in 1891, but the great move towards a systematic training for social workers was made in 1897 when Mary Richmond urged the setting up of a 'school of applied philanthropy' where a faculty would evolve teaching methods that would link theory with practice. The school was established in New York the following year and was extended in 1903 (Bernstein, 1942). It is of interest to note that during that phase the workers were also the students, a model that we would do well to remember. These early teachers in social work were clear that the art of helping people in need required a combination of training which offered knowledge about human behaviour together with the opportunity to apply this in practice with the help of experienced supervisors.

Initially staff supervision developed out of the agency's concern to establish a good service for those in need, and to ensure that available resources were being used appropriately, in conformity with the policies laid down by the local committee or board. These expressed the concern, feeling and prejudice of the day. The use of the word supervision reflects the early emphasis on control and adherence to established policies. Control is still an essential factor in social work supervision owing to statutory responsibilities and the need to adhere to agency policy. With this in mind, the supervisor must define certain boundaries of social work practice. A point at issue at the moment centres around certain kinds of community development work which encourages social action — can this be accommodated in a local authority department or not?

In many settings supervision was first thought of as introducing the fresh worker into the agency. The experienced social worker was given responsibility for inducting the new social worker, who learned directly by accompanying the established worker on visits and by observation of methods. As social work moved from the provision of practical aids to the wider consideration of personal relationships and social interactions, social workers sought opportunities for furthering their knowledge, insights and skills. The educational and enabling elements in supervision were then given recognition and emphasis.

The concept of staff supervision in its totality, embracing the management, teaching and eenabling component, developed slowly in this country and its full application even now is rare. Not many social workers agreed with L. Austin when she wrote in 1952 'Mastery of professional practice in social work represents a continuous period of learning and doing. The supervision of students and staff members therefore differs only as the individual is at a different point in his learning, rather than consisting of the application of a different set of principles and techniques.' Priscilla Young (ISTF 52/22) also makes explicit the 'resistance in the social work services to the idea that field work staff require supervision particularly if they are trained and/or experienced.' At that time many social workers, not least those in specialist fields, considered the suggestion of staff supervision in the nature of an insult, an indication of incompetence to carry out the job for which they had been trained. The kind of supervision that frequently existed in the former children's departments was related to the many statutory obligations that had to be observed and therefore tended towards administrative overseeing rather than towards the kind of teaching that furthers professional development. Sound supervision is provided by individualized teaching and learning on the job and by reflective task-centred discussions. This will provide the stimulus, challenge and work satisfaction that many practitioners find wanting. The local authority's social workers are now asking for this kind of supervision that will help them to function with greater competence and confidence.

The position of the supervisor in departmental structure

The staff supervisor is a key person who looks in two directions, towards the field and towards management; on the one hand being close to the social workers sharing in the provision of client service, and on the other linked to managers and policy makers. The supervisor from her vantage point should know intimately the field's requirements, the calibre of the social workers, how existing resources are being used and the consequences arising from deficiencies. This information is essential to managers evaluating current and future agency resources. This middle or buffer position is potentially uncomfortable on account of differing perceptions by social workers and managers. For example, managers may press for continuous allocation of new cases, although social workers may voice that they already have all they can cope with. The supervisor will have to judge the situation, either declaring upwards and giving evidence that the workers are indeed working to capacity (and not many supervisors find this easy to do), or push down on social workers to take more cases.

The latter occurs with greater frequency. A conscientious supervisor is bound to feel this middle position as a strain.

It follows that preparation and training for this influential role is essential. There is no automatic way by which a social worker of today can become a supervisor by tomorrow. If social service departments aim for effective supervision, the training programme should include preparation for potential supervisors. Be chary of any agency ready to appoint a new supervisor without checking on the applicant's supervisory skills and without preparing adequate facilities for them to carry out the work. It may well be that such an agency will not give the necessary backing to supervisors, or allow effective supervision to be undertaken.

Management elements in supervision

In order to help workers develop their professional skills for the benefit of clients, staff supervisors must strive to obtain suitable conditions for them to work in. 'Room accommodation' rather than 'desk accommodation' for the social worker is required; a quiet atmosphere for reflecting before and after an interview is required. When large numbers of social workers are housed in one room, the chatter of colleagues, the constant ringing of telephones and the far-off clicking of typewriters affect concentration.

When a social worker has the worry of hunting for an interviewing room before he can see the client, he is hardly in the best frame of mind to conduct a sensitive well-focussed interview and to provide the atmosphere and privacy in which a constructive dialogue can take place.

Clients too need to be welcomed into a cosy waiting room instead of being offered a seat in a draughty passage. Poor accommodation negates the very core of social work philosophy with its insistence on human dignity.

The new social worker, apprehensive about conducting an interview, is greatly undermined by such conditions. Such circumstances do not permit the exercise of professional judgment; for example, when it it timely for the client to make the effort himself of coming to the agency rather than to be automatically visited. Client progress is thus in danger of being stunted. It is in her capacity of manager that the supervisor has to declare upwards the consequences of this state of affairs on both social workers and clients, and to push for improvements.

The supervisor must also see that there is the administrative back-up to enable sound practice; for example, there must be clerical provision for adequate recording.

While these matters are essentially the concern of the organization's policy-makers, it may well fall to the supervisor to declare poor conditions and work towards improvement. Communicating upwards the consequences of unsatisfactory work conditions will not make her popular.

Managers do not necessarily have the same perception and may prefer people who do not bring too many difficulties to their attention. Yet it is the supervisor's responsibility to review work conditions. She must also be aware of exaggerations about work conditions being used to excuse poor quality work. Hence the supervisor has to be clear-headed, perceptive, far-seeing, robust and tenacious, and must not mind too much if what she says is displeasing to one side or the other. She must be prepared to declare what cannot be done, state the reasons and produce the evidence; she must also see that possible tasks are implemented. This requires knowledge of the individual's workload, an overview of all the cases and understanding of a social worker's capacity and skill. In these circumstances the allocation of cases to a group of social workers becomes a skilled process where consideration is given to client need and worker skill.

The teaching element in supervision
Learning on the job has to continue at all stages of professional development. Social work courses give basic knowledge and skills, stimulate interest and prepare the ground for integrating theory and practice. The application and consolidation of this learning must take place in subsequent work experience.

Since the social worker in the social services department has to serve a wide range of clientele, and is not able to concentrate on groups of clients with similar pathology, the consolidation of knowledge is a slow process for the newly qualified worker. Generally speaking, there is insufficient opportunity for the new worker to extend what he has learnt from one case to others; he can particularize about one case but since there is only limited opportunity to carry over learning to other similar cases he is handicapped in developing an organized body of knowledge and a working hypothesis. Thus, for a considerable span of time he has to function with a higher degree of uncertainty than did his predecessors who became familiar more quickly with certain categories of clients or problems.

Upon completion of a course the social worker will have been presented with an assortment of complex theoretical concepts together with a wide-ranging, yet limited, practice experience. The student may have had just one experience of dealing with a fostering situation, just one of a mental health problem; one experience of helping an elderly person, one of dealing with a retarded child; he will have learned something about the whole gamut of human misery but in too general a way. Beyond this, today's social work student is expected to have knowledge and/or experience of more than one method of social work intervention. Yet educationalists know that there are very definite limits to how much can be absorbed.

The structure of social work courses makes it essential for departments to create opportunities which allow for integration of theory and practice thus speeding up the period in which the new social worker can begin to practise with a feeling of adequacy. This may be done through the skilled supervisor, who can back up what is missing in the limited experience of the new social worker. More than ever, the staff supervisor has to be a bridge between the knowledge acquired on the course and its application in practice. When so much has yet to be learned, the art of teaching becomes very important. The supervisor has to get a balance between putting in and drawing out; putting in what is not known yet is essential to immediate practice; drawing out what is already known to the worker. Both require understanding of the worker, sensitivity and appropriate timing. This balancing is a highly skilled process. Too little teaching can produce anxiety in the worker who may be afraid to admit that he does not know, while too much input may well stop the worker from thinking for himself, using his own initiative and experience and becoming too dependent on the supervisor and others. The supervisor has to start from the worker's own experience. The worker will bring equipment from his previous setting that can be applied usefully in the new environment and especially when this has been recognized by both supervisor and worker. An illustration in Chapter 5 describes this and emphasizes that however unfamiliar the setting some familiar features are also present. Difficulty arises, however, when the worker is both limited in knowledge and skill and also unable to extend feeling. The supervisor's dilemma is how to enable the worker to learn and become a useful social worker while at the same time ensuring that the client's need for help is being met. The supervisor has a double responsibility; giving attention to client need but also to worker capacity. When the gap between these is too wide it causes realistic concern to the supervisor; in the subsequent pages excerpts from a supervisor's record will highlight this kind of situation when the supervisor is pulled in two directions; hearing the client's plea for help and knowing that the worker's very limited capacity cannot be extended overnight.

Bertha Reynolds' (1963) discourse with Professor Kimball, who was Dean at Smith's College whilst she was teaching there, illuminates the difficulty of achieving the right balance in teaching.

> Professor Kimball put it this way in some of our many talks about educational theory. He agreed that education should not be 'stuffing geese for slaughter', and that too often in academic institutions, it was ... He said, however, that if education means drawing out and leading forth there has to be something put in first. Could I not give the students more and then draw it out? My query was: Wouldn't it then be only what I had given returned and not their own? My

educational theory went wrong, I now believe, for two reasons. First, and obviously, my own theory of social case work was too undeveloped to lend itself to lecture presentation, and my strong belief in the discussion method of teaching was partly a defence against the poverty of my own equipment. Another reason is subtler but, I now believe, a concomitant of the kind of person I was. My greatest intellectual asset has been that all my life I have been a ruminating animal, spending probably two to four hours out of the twenty-four in weaving a mesh of associations around each day's experiences. It has meant an integration of living, a thorough digestion of experience, a richness of association that has been invaluable in teaching as well as in writing and in sheer enjoyment of hours alone. Perhaps this habit was started by a childhood without adequate social stimulation, with long hours of swinging in a hammock in sight of natural beauty. Whatever its origin, once it was part of me I took it for granted that everyone desired to think things over much as I. If I had experienced a good deal of repression, I inferred that others had too, and would seize eagerly an opportunity to bring out their own thoughts in a sympathetic group.

The error Miss Reynolds refers to relates to the mistaken assumption that patterns of learning and living are universally similar. At a later period she paid ample regard to the idiosyncratic nature of a learner's response.

The meaning of support in supervision

Learning cannot easily be accomplished without support. With support the worker can be open and reflective about what he does know but can also acknowledge without loss of face what he does not know. It is easier to make progress once the areas for further learning have been defined and accepted. Support enables the learner to evaluate past practice, consider innovations and alternative approaches.

So often support in social work has come to mean that whatever the other person does or says is not commented on, is certainly not challenged and apparently tolerated. This is not what is meant here. Indeed, the supervisor supports by asking challenging questions about the worker's performance, by stimulating his thinking, and by the very recognition that the worker has the strength and the capacity to respond and develop. Support certainly does not imply blind agreement with what a worker says, thinks or does. It comes from the supervisor's attitude, from the acceptance of another human being, from acknowledging personal assets and limitations and subsequently from an enjoyment in seeing others develop, without feelings of rivalry. Support also derives from a commitment to and a profound interest in the task of helping clients. Such an attitude will transmit itself to the worker who will accept the questions for what they are, and recognize the supervisor's interest in the client, in the task and in himself.

The worker also needs to be sustained through the strains and stresses that arise from the nature of the work and from seeing others suffer. Support is needed especially when clients' problems ring particular bells for the worker, mirror current feelings or reactivate past experiences. Backing and rational thinking are also required when pressures of an organizational nature bear down upon the worker. The opportunity to discuss and share these with an understanding but realistic supervisor can make all the difference to the quality of help offered to clients.

When a social worker's load becomes too heavy, some method of lightening it has to be found. If no support is available, or additional demands are made, the load will be dropped for the sake of survival. Social workers, however, are on the whole conscientious people who care for others and who are only too aware of their responsibility; hence the off-loading does not often take place on a conscious level but occurs in more subtle ways. This can take the form of not hearing, of shutting off, or adopting stereotype practice, of fragmentation, or the use of other mechanisms of defence. Even with support the social worker's task may still be too massive and he may be driven to reduce the task to more manageable proportions. The splitting up of total family problems into concrete tasks to lighten the social worker's load is not a new phenomenon but is believed to occur now with greater frequency because of the social worker's colossal task. The following example illustrates this point:

> The S family will find themselves without a home in a few weeks' time and the social worker has been asked to help in finding accommodation. The social worker's task is to steer the family through this difficult period not only with the practical solution of finding accommodation, but also helping the family to come to terms emotionally with leaving their present locality, friends and neighbours, giving up the only home the family has ever known in this country. This means enabling them to work through feelings of loss and separation, sadness and resentment, before they can begin to face the new situation.

As housing provision is totally inadequate, the social worker is burdened with an impossible task in finding accommodation. His own anxiety, coupled with the intense despair of the family, induces in him also feelings of helplessness.

The social worker's way out is to ignore the family's feelings and to focus on the practical problems, approaching appropriate people by telephone or letters. The social worker is surprised to meet with hostility from the clients despite his active efforts, and eventual success in finding accommodation although he knows from his own experience that he can get angry or depressed when his own strong feelings are disregarded. Theoretically he knows the outcome of this situation is dependent on the factors; practical help but also recognition and sharing of the emotional factors.

In such a case the supervisor needs to be alert to these situations and through discussions help the worker empathize whilst also supporting his practical effort. Since, however, supervisors are also human, and have acted in similar ways themselves and experienced these feelings of helplessness, there is danger of collusion. This occurs when the supervisor views the client's problem in the same way as the worker, because the sympathy between them is based on the latter's identification with the worker's difficulties resembling those experienced by her. The supervisor is therefore unable to help the worker to be objective. Her thinking, like his, has become submerged in mutual feelings towards self protection, and she no longer functions in accord with her role. While the supervisor is in agreement with the worker's actions for reasons of her own, the worker is in fact unsupported and does not receive the necessary stimulus or challenge for his professional development.

Encouraging objectivity

All social workers have on occasions experienced difficulties in maintaining objectivity and rational thinking in relation to particular cases or problems. At times feelings and attitudes get in the way of analytical thinking. The conscious cultivation of self awareness can counteract the tendency towards subjectivity.

The difficulty of remaining objective when the observer is studying material of which he himself is a part is fully discussed by Karl Popper (1972). It is not easy to bring objectivity to bear upon the self. Particular complications arise when the social worker has personal experience of problems which now face his client. In this situation conflicts from the worker's past can be reactivated. Much of the strain inherent in social work comes from this source. To be objective while analysing the situation and at the same time to have the ability to enter into the client's feelings and so to come as near as possible to comprehend the other's situation, is social work practice of the highest order. A supervisor can help the worker to focus on the client yet is also alert to the worker's response and will share the concern or the pain arising from new insights.

The social work profession has always stressed the importance of developing self understanding; since the self is used as an instrument to help others, self recognition is crucial and safeguards must be used to ensure that as far as possible there is no confusion about the feelings that belong to the client and those that belong to the worker. Psychoanalysts, through a personal analysis, aim at self understanding and awareness of their behaviour and feeling in work with patients. Social workers use supervision as an instrument to facilitate greater awareness and control of feeling. Gordon Hamilton (1951) puts it this way:

> In any of the professions aiming to help people, knowledge of the self is essential for the conscious use of the relationship. If one is to use the self, then one must be aware of how the self operates. Not only should the caseworker know something of his motivation for choosing this profession but he must also surmount another hurdle by recognizing his own subjectivity, prejudices and biases. Learning to diagnose involves understanding not only of the client's feelings but also one's own, that is, as distinct from the client's.

All social workers need to maintain empathic understanding and avoid blunting their feelings. The latter occurs where professionals of all kinds work in situations of human stress without adequate support. It also occurs when people have worked in the same or similar organizations for considerable periods of time, have become part of the organizational culture which is by no means always sensitive to the needs of vulnerable clients. For example, a young child refusing to enter a crowded room for purposes of clinical teaching was considered by consultants to be behaving abnormally since most children had conformed to this institutional practice while he had not. Readers can probably draw on their own experience and remember practices to which they took exception when first entering the social services department but to which after a period of time they have become accustomed.

G. Caplan (1959) and I. Menzies (1960) in their respective writings draw attention to the way in which the medical and nursing professions have tended to function in the absence of appropriate support when faced with situations of intense human stress. Caplan comments that when the medical student first enters medical school he has the same kind of readiness to enter into personal relationships as any other person but that by the fourth year his sensitivity has become blunted and he has learned to depersonalize people. He cites the former head of the mental health division of the World Health Organization as saying that his role would be achieved if he could arrange matters so that doctors all over the world would be as sensitive to people as the man in the corner grocery store normally is.

> This lack of sensitivity on the part of doctors is a bad thing but is understandable. These young men come into clinical work in their third year and are suddenly faced with people who have all kinds of problems. If they remain sensitive to the problem, if they allow themselves to be affected by the problems, many of them would break down or would be so upset emotionally that they would not be able to learn. If you look carefully at the techniques of medical education, you will find that in the third year students are brought into contact with physicians who teach them that people are not people at all but biochemical systems. Soon these highly scientific teachers become the students' role models. From this comes a blunting which enables the medical student to go on and learn all kinds of things about the various systems without being upset by the fact that this man is dying or that this one has a family of six children and so on. The medical student does not have to identify himself with those men and so avoids difficulty.

He then comments on the supeervisory model in social work education and describes the aim rather than present common practice when he says:

> Social workers have ways of dealing with similar situations. In schools of social work steps are taken to make sure that the workers remain sensitive in their inter-personal relationship but this is accomplished by means of a very elaborate system for picking up the casualties before they become real casualties. Students are helped over the various crises as they arise; in other words, there is a supervisory system which produces as a finished product someone who remains as sensitive to inter-personal relationship as they were before, and someone who has not 'broken down'. It seems that some medical schools are now patterning themselves on this model by introducing individual supervision.

Menzies (1960) in her study on the nursing service makes similar observations, and explains that a nurse's fragmented tasks in hospital are so arranged to protect her from the extreme anxiety arising from the stressful nature of the work. She comments:

> The nursing service attempts to protect her from the anxiety by splitting up her contact with patients. It is hardly too much to say

that the nurse does not nurse patients. The total workload of a ward or department is broken down into lists of tasks, each of which is allocated to a particular nurse. She performs her patient-centred tasks for a large number of patients, perhaps as many as all the patients in the ward, often thirty or more in number. As a corollary, she performs only a few tasks for and has restricted contact with any one patient. This prevents her from coming effectively into contact with the totality of any one patient and his illness and offers some protection from the anxiety this arouses

These researches demonstrate what happens when members of the caring profession are expected to deal with severe human suffering without the necessary support and when the offered model is one of depersonalization. These experiences are relevant in the present large organization of the social services departments, when there is already a tendency to become too centred on concrete tasks and to pay insufficient regard to relevant feelings and the meaning of personal relationships. Too often clients are expected to discuss their problems with a variety of workers. Yet it is acknowledged that people develop, modify and adjust through personal relationships, be these mother-child, wife-husband or client-worker ones. The supervisory model here is of crucial importance when it can give a living example of a facilitating relationship. It has been shown in social work that those who receive care and understanding are better able to offer it to others.

3 The skills of the supervisor

The need for a change in attitude to supervision
Supervisory practice is not always taken seriously. It is not unknown for a newly qualified student to leave a social work course and to become a student supervisor two months later. On occasions a seconded worker on return has been given the position of senior social worker and expected to supervise others before being given a chance to consolidate her own learning. It still happens that when, after a year's work in an agency, a social worker becomes apathetic, the remedy is sometimes seen in providing him with a student, presumably as a stimulant! The worst example was that of a social worker whose work was judged to be so poor that efforts were made to counsel him out of social work altogether, yet the following day was offered a student. Could he seriously be thought capable of educating someone into a profession from which he himself was now being counselled out?

One might well wonder about such an organizational double-bind, but much more important than this is the poor value and low estimation that has become attached to the highly skilled practice of social work supervision. It is hoped that this publication will clarify the skills required for purposeful supervision and demonstrate that not every Tom, Dick or Harry has the capacity or necessary skill to undertake this very responsible function.

There is in general much ignorance about the nature and the process of supervision, with its major objective of bringing about an effective client service. Social workers who overnight find themselves promoted to the position of supervisors receive little help, if any, with their new functions and tasks. Mostly they are not secure enough to declare their needs for further education in this sphere, afraid of being considered incompetent. This fear, which appears to pervade a large sector of the social work profession, is, I believe, made conscious use of by many organizations who demand the impossible of many senior staff, expecting them to function in new and demanding roles without further educational equipment for these new responsibilities.

Conditions required for sound supervision
The quality of supervision is dependent on three major factors:

1. the agency's understanding and sanctioning of the principles and practice of supervision
2. the supervisor's capacity
3. the worker's capacity.

Two of these will be considered here; the worker's capacity will also be discussed in other sections.

The sanction of the agency, wherein the supervision takes place, is all important in establishing the right climate for supervision. The agency must be clear about its objectives and how these can be achieved, and must believe that good supervision improves the quality of social work practice. The supervisor needs the cooperation of colleagues at all levels; supervision cannot be carried out in isolation. The agency must allow her adequate time. Supervisory sessions should be regular and planned, the duration depending on a worker's stage of development and his pattern of learning. With the worker who is new to the setting it may be better to utilize the two hours of available time by having a planned one-hour unit at the beginning and another one in the middle of the week, while a session of one-and-a-half hours throughout the week may be sufficient for a worker at a different stage of development. Time is needed to prepare and to read the worker's write-up before the session. In addition, the supervisor herself needs a planned period of time to up-date her knowledge.

The staff supervisor's primary function is supervision and other linked activities like allocation of cases; her work with clients is of secondary importance but necessary to the task of supervising. It is essential that the supervisor should be a practising field worker, in order to keep in close touch with the skill she teaches, but she can only carry a limited and selected caseload if she is going to be available to the workers at planned regular sessions. She can be aided by agency procedures, such as standardized requirements for keeping case records. Any underpinning of social work practice by the agency helps the supervisory task and it becomes more effective when it is part and parcel of agency philosophy and procedure.

Agencies which take supervision seriously enable learning opportunities for supervisors. The agency should ensure that supervisory skills go on developing. This can be facilitated by seminar discussions on supervision or by individual consultation from someone with expertise in this field. Preferably it should be both. Much can be achieved by means of seminar groups for supervisors. Looking together at the task of supervising, sharing experiences, considering ways of achieving objectives, discussing alternative ways of helping a worker, giving mutual support with what is still a new task, and last but not least having the opportunity to say in a group of colleagues, 'I don't know', are activities that have great educational and survival value. Stimulation derives from group interchange when participants are gaining experience in having their contributions valued by colleagues and in turn acknowledging theirs. There is much joy and excitement in shared learning.

Individual consultation on supervision (see Chapter 9 'Consultation') provides a different means of sharing and learning; it has been used by supervisors in those rare organizations where it is available.

Consultation allows for an individual approach to learning and permits the supervisor, now also consultee, to continue with detailed explorations of complex situations over more than one session if necessary, in a manner that suits her. This would be possible in the group situation only if the other participants were equally interested in the minutiae of that particular aspect. When both methods of learning exist side by side, group seminars tend to be especially useful when common factors in learning are being considered, while individual consultations tend to be used more to discuss details of individual practice. It would appear that consultations are more consciously used to clarify a supervisor's perplexity about her own way of operating than are the seminars; however, this is not always the case and depends on the encouragement and interest shown by other seminar members. It is useful for an organization to make provisions for both methods of learning; these complement each other. An added advantage to the supervisor is that consultation is available during periods when there are no seminar groups in progress. The importance that an agency gives to supervision can be assessed by the further learning facilities it provides for staff supervisors.

The capacity and skills of the supervisor

Staff supervision is one of the few learning opportunities available to the social worker. How real this opportunity is will depend on the capacity of the supervisor.

Supervisors are made very quickly in the post-Seebohm era; this is due to a variety of factors, some of which have been elaborated in Chapter 1. It also relates to the general ignorance of the function of supervision, the necessary skills and the poor understanding of professional maturation. The supervisor must in the first place have competence in the area in which she teaches. Competence derives from the fusion of theoretical knowledge and practical application over some years of practice in the field, especially when the development of skills has been underpinned by the kind of supervision that leads to an increase of understanding of the many complex factors inherent in human living. It is evident that when the supervisor has to pay too much attention to her learning needs, her focus cannot be as it should, on the social worker and his task of helping clients. 'The ability to impart knowledge,' writes L. Austin (1952), 'is in principle related to the possession of knowledge. The bedside manner is not a substitute for proficiency in the physician or the social worker or the teacher.'

This simple truth does not always seem to be appreciated by organizations or indeed by applicants for supervisory posts. It only acquires meaning when the social worker, finding herself in this position, feels unable to acknowledge her lack in supervisory equipment, since being in the post apparently suggests that she has what it takes. Her dilemma is real. Unless she has the courage to declare what learning opportunities she requires to function adequately in her new role, she will be forced to live in a make-believe situation, probably for much of her professional life. Whilst she will have to endure much, those below her will also lose substantially. Many professional social workers of good potential are now in danger of becoming stunted in their professional development by being propelled upwards prematurely, and in their turn will impede the development of others. It takes a person of great stature to manage to extricate herself from this unhealthy situation and to get off the upward moving escalator.

The great human cost to the client, the supervisee and the supervisor, when the latter is prematurely appointed to a supervisory position, often without provision for further learning, makes it advisable to discuss some of the basic requirements for becoming a supervisor.

Supervision does not mean telling people what to do, though it is often seen and indeed practised in this way. Supervision is an individualized method of learning further in the performance of a responsible job. To help people learn, to ask questions in a way which leads to well considered and appropriate decisions, calls for theoretical knowledge, practical skills and experience as a competent social worker. The requirements for furthering knowledge are:

1. the possession and consolidation of knowledge
2. teaching skill
3. empathy for colleagues and clients
4. enjoyment in the development of others
5. familiarity with agency structure
6. an ability to regulate emotional pressures
7. appropriate use of authority
8. willingness to develop.

These criteria will be discussed below.

1 THE POSSESSION AND CONSOLIDATION OF KNOWLEDGE

The supervisor must have skill in study and diagnosis and establish a feasible treatment plan; i.e. she will be able to apply a wide range of social work and interviewing techniques suited to the client. Knowledge about human behaviour and motivation at different stages of development and in different situations is essential.

A supervisor must also be acquainted with the normal anxiety that occurs in learning, the normal dependency that happens in new situations and the different ways of behaving when people find themselves in learning situations. The supervisor must be familiar with established stages of learning and be ready to study the individual learning patterns of workers. John Dewey's message (1963) might have been specially written for supervisors: 'Teaching carries with it the responsibility for understanding the needs and capabilities of the individuals who are learning at a given time. It is not enough that certain materials and methods have proved effective with other individuals at other times. It is important to pay attention to what is education with particular individuals at particular times. There is no such thing as educational value in the abstract.'

Socrates would have made an excellent supervisor; he understood how to develop a stimulating dialogue between pupils and teacher, could encourage alternative ways of thinking, could draw forth the knowledge that was his pupils', develop further their thinking, and create enjoyment and enthusiasm amongst his learners. He did not tend towards authoritative statements that could have closed the door to further explorations and discoveries. His approach was always positive, though critical. Supervision has much in common with this method of teaching, with the shared task, the active part in learning, the conviction that whilst certain knowledge should be imparted to the learner, the way he will integrate and use it will be essentially his own. Hence the didactic approach to teaching in social work does not commend itself.

Being competent in social work does not imply that mastery in all areas of social work could possibly be achieved, though thorough knowledge related to certain subject matters could be expected. No one could have skill and experience in the wide range of human needs that social workers are now called upon to help. The supervisor should, however, be clear where her competence ends, so that whenever necessary she can get help from another source for the worker. It takes a competent supervisor, however, to know and declare her limits without apology.

2 TEACHING SKILL

Teaching, enabling others to gain further competence, is an important supervisory skill (see also Chapter 5). The ability to impart knowledge or direct a worker to the source of knowledge at an appropriate time, i.e. when he can put it to immediate use, is of highest importance. Exploration skills are perhaps the least developed of all supervisory equipment. Exploratory skill means posing questions that stimulate the other person to reflect and consider alternative means of proceeding. Why are these skills so rare in supervision? Does their lack relate to attitude or to lack of the supervisor's knowledge and skill? It is often suggested that when questions are asked like, 'Why did you do this? What led you to do that?' that this implies negative criticism. Many supervisors therefore do not ask these questions, either from fear of producing an uncomfortable atmosphere in supervision or because they lack the necessary understanding and knowledge to ask such questions. Frequently it is not known what was at the back of a worker's mind when making certain comments or proposing certain actions. When asked, a supervisor may guess or 'assume', when it would have been quite simple to ascertain what prompted a worker's specific comment.

Far from disliking being questioned many social workers say that they would welcome exploratory enquiry and the kind of challenging that would lead to greater stimulation and interest in work. It does seem that both the supervisor's attitude and uncertainty of her social work competence are responsible for this scarce teaching skill. This relates, of course, to the supervisor's readiness to take on the responsibility to supervise, and this she cannot do with any degree of comfort unless she has been able to consolidate her own knowledge and skill since qualification. Yet with the present shortage of skilled supervisors this is often the case. The strain of being responsible for someone else's work when unsure of meeting one's own responsibility must indeed by very great.

One of the most important considerations in teaching is to take serious note of what any one worker can absorb at any one time, and not to veer away from this under any circumstances. It is a common failing not only amongst supervisors but teachers of all kinds to teach too much and not to see the 'halt' sign. The teacher may well feel that by teaching all, he has discharged his obligations; but, on the contrary, too much material causes barriers to be erected against the massive input. To be clear about what needs to be taught in what order is the requisite of a good supervisor; she must therefore ascertain what a beginning social worker knows and then sort out what she can provide to maximize the service he can give at that particular time.

The supervisor must give shape to a supervisory session. There should be a beginning, a middle and an end. It is good practice to plan how to use the limited discussion time. It happens frequently that neither supervisor nor worker takes responsibility for this and both have a sense of dissatisfaction at the end of an unfocussed and unplanned session. It has been suggested that the so-called informality makes for a comfortable relationship. I believe that this is not so but is more likely to produce feelings of frustration because what has been achieved remains vague. It is also a poor work model for client work, when supervisor and worker cannot be clear by the end of the session what has been the focus of their discussion and what the outcome.

Another important teaching function of the supervisor, especially following qualification, is the bridge-building work that has to occur between theoretical concepts learned in the classroom and their application in the field. The supervisor in the social services department has to help make these concepts real, to bring them to life and to understand their origin. Left to his own devices the new worker would probably relate the erratic attendances of a client to his own limited knowledge and lack of confidence rather than to the existence of ambivalence, of which he may have theoretical knowledge but not have had the opportunity to recognize in practice.

Similarly the concept of transference only acquires meaning when it can be seen to operate in the interview situation. The irrational behaviour of clients, often perceived as hostility, might well be countered by an inexperienced worker with irritation, annoyance, or even withdrawal from the case. When in the supervisory session this is seen as a transference reaction relating to someone in the past whom the client links with the person of the worker, he may then be able to respond in a helpful way to the client. At a more basic level, the staff supervisor has to explore with the beginning worker what may underly a stereotyped client request which after all gives him entry to the social services; this clarification is necessary with an inexperienced worker especially in an overstretched department where important exploratory questions are rarely asked.

Insignificant details only partly perceived take on more meaning in discussion with an interested supervisor. The words 'manipulative client' that seem to have crept into social work literature, also need careful examination. These are generally used when a client's legitimate demands cannot be met by the worker. When recently a supervisor inquired further about this term, it seemed thoroughly misapplied:

> A teenage girl placed in an assessment centre, rejected by her mother, had a strong wish to visit the mother. This could only be achieved by the social worker taking her to the mother's home some

distance away. The girl's need for reassurance was very great and she had phoned her mother to say the worker would bring her over that day. When she informed the worker of this, the latter was furious, annoyed, asking resentfully how this girl dared to attempt to control her time. She was completely oblivious of the needs of this very deprived girl.

The worker could not have taken the girl to see her mother that day because of other commitments, but her own angry feelings had completely obliterated this girl's urgent need and made it impossible for her to be constructive. For the worker to gain awareness of her own outraged feelings and how she had placed these onto the client, and then to understand the effects of her behaviour on the client, was no simple matter and required a secure supervisory relationship where insight could be developed. This, and other instances of a similar nature, have reinforced my view that when social workers talk so much about manipulative clients nowadays, it is not that their number has increased but rather that there has been a decrease in the quality of good supervision.

3 EMPATHY FOR COLLEAGUES AND CLIENTS

Any teacher needs to be interested both in his subjects and in those he teaches. The supervisor needs to be genuinely interested in the mental health and welfare of the client and be able to convey this in the supervisory session. A supervisor who lacks this basic requirement may still be a useful adviser, may know about techniques of interviewing and methods of intervention, but will lack the vital part of human concern and caring so that much of the substance is missing. It is unlikely that such a supervisor can greatly motivate the worker in the total helping process. Those who as case workers have lacked interest in their clients do not make good supervisors. Equally, supervisors who continue to be mainly interested in what happens to clients also do not make good supervisors.

The supervisor will have to come to terms with the fact that her primary function has changed from helping clients directly to helping the worker to help the client; she also will have to accept the fact that she can often see how a client could be more readily helped if certain skills were available to the worker but at that stage are still beyond his reach. She can support, encourage and indicate the right direction, but finally has to accept that the worker can do no more than his best. This is never easy to achieve for committed practitioners, but it is especially difficult when a supervisor feels more at home in her former role as social worker than in the present supervisory one. The wish to take over can be understood but must nevertheless be resisted. She needs flexibility and self discipline to carry this through.

4   ENJOYMENT IN THE DEVELOPMENT OF OTHERS

To provide learning opportunities for others, the supervisor must enjoy seeing others develop and finally become independent. This requires a mature attitude and one that lacks feelings of competition and rivalry. In a similar way to a parent, she shares gladly in the achievement and progress but also stands by at moments of discouragement and failure. Such an attitude can enable the worker to recognize his strength yet at the same time help him to acknowledge the less developed areas. A supervisor whose feet are firmly rooted in practice can do this. She does not have to demonstrate her superior knowledge by denigrating the worker. This inner security cannot be expected of supervisors who have allowed themselves to be forced into this position after perhaps only a year's qualification.

Some new supervisors who are understandably unsure of their contributions to supervision after only a short period in the field, are inclined to perceive mainly the worker's weaker areas in an attempt to demonstrate superior knowledge, while others deal with their uncertainty by avoiding sessions, or by an absence of questioning or by too easy agreement with the worker's proposed action. Their own uncertainty makes it difficult to elucidate alternative ways of helping.

This does not mean that the experienced supervisor will not naturally continue to learn; it is never possible to achieve total understanding of the uniqueness of human nature or gain mastery of practice in the wide arena of social work where environmental conditions change frequently. But this is learning of a different kind and does not clash with the needs of the worker.

5   FAMILIARITY WITH AGENCY STRUCTURE

A confident supervisor is firmly based in the agency. Familiarity with agency climate, with the nature of referrals, with the geographical conditions, with the procedures of the agency, knowledge of resource people and the significant people in the agency, are all necessary for the supervisor to carry her responsibilities. It is difficult for a supervisor to function immediately in a new setting even if she has been in a supervisory job previously.

6   AN ABILITY TO REGULATE EMOTIONAL PRESSURES

In most supervisory sessions the unsatisfactory life situation or relationships of clients forms a large part of the material for discussion from which better understanding of complex situations can be gained. Since the subject matter relates either to environmental hardship or to personal and interpersonal conflict, feelings are in the forefront and play a large part in any possible resolution of conflict. It is to be expected that these will at times stimulate in the worker remembrances of long forgotten episodes, bring to the fore memories which will result in the worker's subjective ruminations, preoccupations and responses. The client's problem may therefore arouse emotional responses in the worker. While the process of helping people makes use of theoretical knowledge and understanding, the nature of the task also brings into the situation emotional implications. It is not possible to prescribe in general for such occurrences. A supervisor who knows the worker may understand the nature of these responses and know what in this instance would be most helpful. She must assess when focussing attention on the essential problem of the client and away from the worker's own concerns is appropriate; or when it would be more help to attend, if only for a time, to the worker's preoccupations. There is a very delicate balance between well-timed theoretical input and the acknowledgment of the emotional impact. The latter can increase the worker's personal awareness and make for greater availability to his clients. On the other hand, too much preoccupation with the self can have the opposite effect and lead to an emotional withdrawal from the client to whom he would no longer be a helper. It is essential in these complex situations that the supervisor also has someone available for discussion.

7 APPROPRIATE USE OF AUTHORITY

The supervisor needs to maintain dual focus; this requires her to consider the needs of the case and also the skill of the worker. A feasible treatment plan must include assessment of the quality of help the worker can offer. The supervisory sessions should be used to discuss alternative ways of helping. These should enable him to elect with greater confidence his own approach; this may differ from the precise way the supervisor would herself deal with the case. Social work competence, humility and wisdom are required to allow the worker to follow his own course when his way appears just as appropriate. On occasions risks may be involved and readiness to take these should come from the supervisor's understanding of the case and the worker's capacity, knowledge of a client's resilience and the nature of the defences; not from ignorance or lack of interest. The supervisor cannot do the worker's learning for him and has to allow him to experiment and find his own way of dealing with a given situation.

With the readiness to take risks goes the ability to contain anxiety: the worker's, when he feels that nothing is going right, and the supervisor's when unsure about a worker's way of going about his work. At times the supervisor's anxiety may be fully justified and may require a different decision from the one taken by the worker. This step presents difficulties for many supervisors; it seems easier to give the workers their head even when this is clearly not in the interest of the client. At times there appears to exist some kind of collusion; the supervisor would wish to be allowed to operate in the same permissive kind of way by his superior and this engenders a kind of fellow feeling and permits the worker to act unchallenged in his way. In general, there is reluctance to be firm; this may be related to a supervisor's uncertainty, to not knowing when it is appropriate to be firm and when a worker has to be held to a commitment. Even in a case when the client's severe depression was fully recognized by a competent supervisor though not understood by the worker, the supervisor had the greatest difficulty in instructing the worker to visit the client frequently and regularly over this critical period of time. Such instructions should, of course, always be followed up later by appropriate discussion and necessary teaching.

Firmness is often welcomed by workers particularly by those who feel insecure and especially when this is given by a supervisor who normally is very ready to let the worker discover his own way. Indeed the occasional demonstration of firmness will enable the worker to extend this to clients when this becomes necessary. There is much to be discussed around this area of authority, the difficulty of using it and the degree to which the supervisor herself has resolved her own attitude towards authority.

Many supervisors deny that there is an element of authority in supervision. Some avoid making firm decisions or giving instructions which are necessary for the protection of clients. In some cases this inability arises from uncertainty as to whether the instruction would be carried out and also what degree of backing could be expected from superiors. There is a general feeling that the use of authority, giving directives, making decisions, drives a wedge into relationships and makes for unpopularity.

There are then personal and organizational reasons why the appropriate use of authority tends to get shelved. On the personal front, the need to be liked and accepted, and to feel part of a group in a large organization, especially when working with distressed and disturbed people in society, becomes very urgent. Reluctance to accept authority derives also from organizational uncertainties. Many social services departments have not clarified how this responsibility is perceived and what authority is allocated to this role. Supervisors are told that they are responsible for the worker's functioning but it is often left very unclear what organizational backing would be given if supervisory authority were challenged. The supervisor needs to know precisely what responsibility is entailed in her job and what authority is required to fulfil her commitment. It seems that some senior staff are ambivalent about the delegation of authority to supervisors which causes confusion and discomfort. When this occurs the supervisor attempts to carry out her job, but in a haze of mystification. Under those circumstances it is not surprising that using authority is avoided when it should be applied. The absence of declared organizational authority needs discussion and clarification within the organization. A supervisor cannot be expected to carry responsibility without clearly defined authority.

A different kind of authority derives also from the supervisor's personal competence to do the job to which she has been assigned. The supervisor who is unsure of her ground will of course experience difficulty in overruling the social worker even on matters that intimately affect the protection of clients.

It is beyond the range of this chapter to go into more refined details about the nature of authority. Some aspects will link up with infantile patterns, the use of authority by parents, the child's reaction. Supervisors who have difficulty in this area may on reflection find that these difficulties are not confined to their work setting. It is important that each supervisor gives consideration to this aspect prior to taking on the role of supervisor when she will be not only responsible for someone else's work but will also be expected to pass judgment. Supervisors should review their own attitudes and responses to authority and at least strive to bring competitive and negative responses under reasonable control. Finally, supervisors must accept that they are not the same as social workers, that they have a different role, a different function, different authority and responsibilities, a different status and salary.

Judgment about whether a worker is ready to supervise must be based on competence in this whole sphere of supervision but must certainly include an assessment of the worker's psychological maturity; particular regard should be paid to a worker's reactions to authority and to assess how able he is to deal with that aspect of the role. Being in authority brings problems for many people; it will unnerve some, while others will pretend it does not exist, and others still will misuse it by demonstrating continually that they are the ones in control.

8 WILLINGNESS TO DEVELOP

The supervisor must herself believe in ongoing learning and progress and enjoy looking further and understanding better. If she does not enjoy learning herself she is unlikely to make a good supervisor. Learning is like living, it is never static and it always moves on. A supervisor who is ready to explore further herself and with the worker is a stimulant and demonstrates that development goes on in and around us. It is extremely helpful to a worker to be told by the supervisor 'I don't know the answer to this but let's see if we can find out together.'

A competent supervisor should have at her disposal a range of teaching skills which can be adapted to the way a worker learns. Everybody has different ways of learning. It is a supervisory responsibility to try and adapt her own teaching to the learning pattern of the worker. Some workers are enabled by a high degree of independent work while others may require much more support and opportunity to think through issues with the supervisor. Most learning proceeds on the basis of stimulation that derives from mutual interchange of ideas. A supervisor should be perceived as someone who enjoys her work and who genuinely believes that the more you know, the more there is still to be known.

In case the new supervisor feels somewhat intimidated by these many requirements, the following chapter deals with the practical issues of supervising the new worker.

4 Some practical issues for new supervisors

Guidelines for a beginning supervisor and a newly qualified worker
The supervisor will be the person responsible for the new worker's work, the person with most frequent and regular contact, and the one to assess what he will contribute to the existing team. Therefore the supervisor should be present at the appointment. The supervisor needs to have information about the worker's background, education and experience, and gain some understanding of his attitudes and skills.

The new worker will equally wish to meet and assess the person to whom he will be accountable and learn something about the pattern of supervision. Already in the appointment interview there should be an attempt to clarify the contract in relation to supervision. In the first supervisory session further discussion is required as to the regularity, the frequency and the general pattern of supervision; about the worker's hopes and expectations of supervision and his past experience of it. The supervisor too needs to declare her understanding of supervision and the priority she allocates to this as against other tasks. This lays the foundation of understanding for the future and creates the necessary climate for it.

In the first few sessions the newcomer is informed about the agency's procedures and practices; about key and resource people in the organization and the manner of communication in the agency. The worker should know and feel that this is his time, his period of uninterrupted replenishment, and therefore phone interrruptions would not be allowed. There should be at least one period in the week for every worker when he can feel that his concerns take priority over all else. This needs to become an established practice in supervision and it is for the supervisor to cultivate it and adhere to this discipline. Lack of interruption is required for concentrated thinking, for the developing of themes and for the persuance of goals. It is also important to demonstrate this model in supervision so that the social worker emulate it in his practice with clients.

From this model workers learn that it is this fixed but unhurried time that enables problems and remedies to be thought through. If this pattern is not established early on in the supervisor/worker relationship, both will at times attempt to extricate themselves from a difficult session. Many a supervisor has at times allowed a worker to forget about a supervision session when both have felt uneasy about a disagreement or feared mutual confrontation, but avoidance does not resolve conflict or difficulties.

It is useful for a beginning supervisor to consider her objectives, to review her whole range of work and then to develop a programme which allows her to fulfil all her functions.

The objectives

The broad objectives of supervision are to develop further knowledge, skill and confidence in the practice of social work, and by these means to provide an adequate service to clients.

There are two main areas for continued discussion in supervision:
1. the casework process in detail and depth
2. the management of the caseload including recognition of a worker's choice of priority cases.

THE CASEWORK PROCESS IN DETAIL AND DEPTH

When the worker and supervisor are looking at a case in detail (whether a crisis one, a long-term family problem case, or one of a practical nature, consideration will be given to the nature of the case, causation and onset, and attention will be paid to the processes of study, diagnosis, planning and treatment. The interaction in the interview, the worker's own responses and techniques as well as the progress of the case will be part of a continued dialogue in supervision.

The supervisor will start where the worker is, and indicate that his work is valued and his uneven contributions acceptable and of use. These will be taken realistically for what they are. When discussing total work performance, good work will be pinpointed as will the need to increase practice skills in certain areas. This underlines the importance of an initial assessment of the worker's capabilities.

Supervisor's skills are called upon to understand what are common difficulties in learning, bearing in mind the possibility also of individual learning blocks. The supervisor's skill in drawing out or putting together for practical purposes what the worker cannot yet know by himself is important. For example, questions like 'tell me about it, how was his mood when he said "I don't need anybody"?', enables the worker to look retrospectively at the interview and he may see aspects that would not otherwise have come to the fore. Clients' comments are suddenly remembered and can take on a wider meaning as these are being discussed. The supervisor's experience can complement the worker's knowledge, so that the client is better understood. For example, the concept of self determination has little meaning when a severely depressed client is expected to make a decision. When her coping capacity is so low the client will require a worker to make decisions for her, for example that she will need a home help when first returning home from hospital. The supervisor has to make explicit the circumstances when basic social work assumptions can be usefully applied and when the application of these would be inappropriate to the client's present needs.

It cannot be stressed enough that the supervisor's concern is with the social worker and his task and not with the social worker and his personal problems. All supervisors need to keep this focus in mind but especially new supervisors who, in their previous assignment, concentrated on the problems of clients. As the new worker will deal with some new referrals the supervisor may wish to pay particular attention to a worker's early contacts with new clients, prepare him for the interview and be available when it comes to piecing together a client's situation. If the supervisor values what the worker can do but at the same time shares with him the areas where skills are lacking, it will help the worker and will also demonstrate an important casework principle, (which can be applied by worker to client), which is, to recognize existing strengths and to provide the right climate for the further development of existing potential. The supervisor will have to consider what understanding the worker has derived from interviews that will be useful to him in building up a psycho-social diagnosis and treatment plan. If the material is scant the supervisor will have to consider why this is so.

Here are some possible reasons why the worker has only scant information about the client:

1. Realistically there has been insufficient time to get to know the client and the situation.
2. The worker may be focussing in too narrow a way on the client's request, shutting off other relevant areas, either because he does not see the connection between related aspects of the case, or, because he is reluctant to explore areas where he may have difficulty in coping.
3. Lack of knowledge or not knowing how to apply it may account for the limited picture of a client's situation.
4. The new worker may have a difficult time handling his own feelings and be fearful of being swamped by client's problems; he may then deal with this by uttering trite comments or offer reassurances that close the door to further discoveries and understanding.

The supervisor should recognize how the worker functions and relate this to his learning pattern. She should reflect whether she could have prepared him to anticipate the clients likely mood and behaviour, knowing more herself about the responses of people in given situations.

THE MANAGEMENT OF THE CASELOAD

The management of a worker's caseload is a complex matter and requires at least initially the supervisor's very active help. How does the worker allocate his time in relation to all his cases in a rational, not a hit and miss, kind of way? This is no easy matter.

Although this area is discussed in a later chapter, some preliminary points will need to be made here. In supervision, the objectives in opening a case in order to help a family should first be established; these should relate to the needs of the family and also to available resources. Only when these have been clarified can the nature of help be determined, the frequency of contact planned and the effectiveness of this help assessed at various periods of time. The new worker should be allowed to build up his caseload gradually, so that he gets a chance to get to know his clients in an unhurried way. He needs time to interview and time for reflection after interview and during supervision. This also allows the supervisor to get intimate knowledge of how this worker understands and helps clients and how he determines priorities in respect of his caseload. Only a few examples will be offered here since supervisors will wish to do their own thinking and bring their own experiences to bear on this important area. Priorities are not always rationally based. They occur because of:

1   organizational demands and statutory requirements
2   pressures from outsiders to act in a particular case
3   the worker s own interest in particular areas of work, i.e. work with children or the elderly
4   the worker's response to a particular client, when, for example, there exists fellow feeling and he may pursue this client to the exclusion of others
5   the worker is being made to feel of use, needed and welcomed
6   clients who have problems that if unattended lead to greater problems.

The supervisor has to understand the worker's way of establishing priorities, to share it with him and hold the balance between different clients' needs and service. Frank discussion has to take place periodically about a worker's particular interests and priorities and the effect on his selection of clients. What weighting should be given to the worker's interests, and how can this be balanced in relation to the total work commitment of the team? These are questions of great importance and call for open discourse with the team. The worker, too, needs to recognize how he established his priorities.

Organizing time
The practical mechanism of giving attention to these important work aspects within regular but limited supervision time needs consideration. The greater the number of tasks, the more care has to be taken in the ordering of these, so that the limited time is utilized appropriately.

The beginning supervisee requires a longer period of supervision time than the more experienced worker. He also requires more guidance and direction. A two-hour period is suggested as an appropriate allocation of time, although in the early stages there will be matters that require immediate discussion and cannot wait until the next supervisory session comes round. The supervisor would do well to hold time in reserve for this purpose.

The supervisor should require a list of clients on the worker's first caseload, stating the referral problem, the subsequent diagnosis, his objectives and methods in dealing with the client, and plans for contact. Supervisor and worker then know the total picture when discussing in detail the needs of the case and the availability of resources for this case alongside other cases who will be considered in similar ways. When there exists an agreed plan and when both supervisor and social worker come prepared to a session, economy of time and effort result. It helps to establish a pattern which will be used most of the time but which can be altered when the need arises. The beginning social worker will usually appreciate a structure that gives some order and certainty in a situation that has so many unknown and unfamiliar features. Thus time could be allocated in the following way:

1 to full detailed case discussions
2 to review some of the cases on the caseload
3 to a preparatory discussion of a new case
4 to other considerations arising out of a week's work
5 to planning some of the discussion points for the next session.

Obviously the time pattern will vary somewhat according to current requirements. Nevertheless it can be very helpful for a worker to know when planning, that forty minutes will be available for a thorough case discussion; half-an-hour will be devoted to a review of some of the cases; twenty minutes can be counted on for a preliminary preparatory discussion of a new case; twenty minutes will be available for raising other works aspects, and that the last ten minutes or so will be devoted to deciding on priorities for the next session. This kind of disciplined structuring is also useful to supervisors who may otherwise pay undue attention to work aspects to which they themselves are especially committed and interested in and to ignore other equally important areas for discussion. It is also considered part of responsible supervision to record, if only briefly, the main content of the session, what has been achieved and what remains left over for future discussions.

Restricted worker capacity; problems for the supervisor

Due to the shortage of competent social work practitioners, unqualified and newly qualified staff find that they are expected to undertake complex work with clients for which they have not been equipped. Supervisors have the equally difficult task of enabling these workers to cope to the best of their abilities. Since many supervisors are now faced with this situation, some issues and dilemmas alluded to earlier will be further highlighted by means of extracts from a supervisor's record.

Mrs R, an unqualified social worker in her twenties, had worked in a welfare department for one year. She had mainly worked with the elderly and her work tasks had been concrete and practical. At no time had she been supervised and what she had learned was from her own efforts. In the new department she had to work with a variety of clients and undertake unfamiliar tasks. Also for the first time she had a supervisor. The newly established department lacked structure and direction and many staff were struggling with new roles and responsibilities. The supervisor too was new to the department though not new to supervision; she also had to find her way around and deal with many frustrations.

Prior to the appointment of the supervisor this particular social worker had been asked to take on a fifteen-year-old girl who had left home and was thought to be at risk. She was the daughter of divorced parents. The girl had been seen in quick succession by a number of social workers and was now to be helped by Mrs R who had no experience of working with teenage girls and who seemed thoroughly at sea.

In the first supervisory session she had expressed hope that the supervisor would give her the formula for handling 'an uncooperative girl'. This label had been gained solely from reading the record, as she had not yet met Betty. Her initial idea was to place Betty where she would be made to conform. She was asked to talk about Betty's background in order to help the supervisor find out how much she knew of this girl's situation. The worker responded by saying scathingly, 'Well, she comes from a split background and her mother is difficult and can be objectionable, but Betty is fifteen, sophisticated and attractive, and modern in dress.' The social worker's disapproval of Betty was evident; all her comments were critical and negative and the supervisor could detect no sympathy whatever for this girl without a home.

It seemed to the supervisor that one of her main functions was helping the social worker to gain some understanding of Betty as a person; without this it was unlikely that the social worker could be of help. The supervisor says here: 'This made me extremely anxious since I was aware that Betty's condition was deteriorating faster than social work help would be forthcoming. Over the next few sessions I found myself explaining Betty to the social worker, trying to establish how Betty was feeling in this situation. It was difficult to know how the worker used this; I noted that the worker frequently returned to the question of Betty's unsuitable lodgings and focussed on the need to find Betty more suitable accommodation. This had been one of the social worker's previous tasks and in this area she generally knew how to proceed.' The supervisor did not share the social worker's concern about these practicalities although she could understand the worker's tendency to want to hang on to what had been to her a familiar activity. The supervisor comments: 'Maybe in my anxiety to help her understand Betty I pressed her too hard, so that she had to return to what for her was familiar practice.'

This is one of the supervisor's dilemmas; the supervisor's genuine concern for the client, her urgency to convey this to an apparently unsympathetic, unknowing worker, and the client's situation in danger of further deterioration. It is on the whole not unnatural to have a first negative reaction to a client who does not arouse immediate sympathy. What is important in supervision is for the worker to understand the reasons for the negative response without provoking too much guilt. This is of course easy to see with hindsight when the pressures of the work are not bearing down upon the supervisor.

Eventually, a departmental decision was taken, largely as the result of the mother's pressure, to bring Betty before the court as being in need of care and protection. Mrs R showed no awareness about what Betty might be feeling, and appeared thoroughly disinterested in how she might respond. The supervisor here carries on: 'Whilst cursing the department for appointing an unqualified social worker who even lacked the capacity to feel for clients, I wondered whether reallocation of the case to another worker would help the situation. I decided at that stage of the case that it would help neither client nor worker.' It should also be noted here that this worker had difficulty in feeling for many clients, only towards the elderly could she extend more understanding.

The supervisor took infinite pains in considering what methods might produce some positive feeling in the worker, and finally decided on what she considered would make an immediate impact which was to encourage the worker to think back to the time when she was Betty's age. In one sense it worked; the social worker began to think herself into the girl's situation, began to feel something about her unfortunate circumstances, began to express anger about the events that had befallen Betty, began to see her not only as the villain but also as the victim.

When, however, it came to the next supervisory session the worker presented a sad picture. The supervisor says: 'The social worker looked distraught, unkempt, quite unlike her usual self and declared with tearful outpouring that she felt unable to cope. She was extremely distressed and with some encouragement from me explained that everything had got on top of her. She was getting behind with her work, she was worrying continuously, she was bothered about the amount of time a single case can take, and how quickly you get behind with routine visits and then other things go wrong. It seemed that the pressure in the last session to make her feel more about Betty had also made her wonder about her other clients and that she had not been doing enough for them.' At this point the supervisor herself felt helpless and in some way experienced herself the burden of this worker.

At the same time this also seemed to indicate a positive step forward. The supervisor now began to express some sympathy for the worker who had some real reason to complain; the department was disorganized, decision making was frequently delayed, all social workers had more to do than they could realistically cope with, and this worker in particular had been expected to work with people in ways she was not able to do. The supervisor now became aware that this caused Mrs R worry and stress. She also began to recognize that Betty was not an easy girl to understand and would have been a difficult case for a more experienced worker; it is not clear however whether the supervisor shared this understanding with the worker at that time, to whom this would have been of help.

Again, at this stage the supervisor realised that the girl was not getting the required help, she still had considerable uncertainty about the potential of this social worker, though recently she had shown slow signs of growth, and it seemed as if for the first time she was gaining understanding of the nature of social work. The supervisor very much wished to help the social worker gain some insight and to discuss with her the nature of the anxiety experienced at times by anybody who is new to a particular job and not certain whether one is proceeding in the right direction. She could see also that the worker had many other duties, and considered it advisable to look at the total caseload and see whether some reduction could be made.

It is of interest that during the period when the social worker felt so unsure in her work she was unable to do even the practical things that at other times had come easily to her; for example, she was no longer able to look for accommodation for Betty in an effective way. It seemed most important to help the worker to regain confidence so that a substantial part of one supervisory session was taken up in exploring jointly the practical possibilities of finding accommodation. The supervisor was concerned about this worker's loss of confidence in areas where she had previously functioned with comfort and could not but wonder whether in her concern for the client she had tried to accelerate the pace of the social worker too much.

Following the court hearing and Betty's admission to an assessment centre, social worker and client developed more contact. Seeing all the family in court had helped the social worker's understanding of the total situation; while Betty herself expressed in her own way some appreciation of the social worker's presence both in court and in settling her into the assessment centre. At this stage the social worker was beginning to listen to Betty, could understand some of her feeling and resentments without herself becoming negative and rejecting. It is of interest to note the supervisor's comments around this time, when she remembered that most of the social worker's previous experience had after all been with old people who were grateful for little comforts she had managed to supply for them; if on rare occasions an old person had been difficult this had been excused on the grounds of age.

Reading the record in retrospect it almost appeared that the supervisor at this period in time was seeing the worker more as an individual than as a helper of others and one could speculate that this brought about in the worker a greater concern for the client. Perhaps this progress could have occurred sooner had the supervisor encouraged the worker to begin with her familiar role!

In due course the social worker developed a pleasant enough relationship with Betty which however remained at a superficial level. Nevertheless, the social worker offered Betty a consistent contact, a certain amount of caring, and at that time she was the only steady person in Betty's life. During the seven months to follow, work continued and some trust developed between worker and client. The worker still tended to concern herself more with practicalities though there was some change in her ability to understand another person. The supervisor still had doubts about this worker's capacity to sustain ongoing relationships and work constructively over periods of time.

For reasons of space and identification it is not possible to quote in greater detail from the records. Nevertheless, there is enough material to pose a number of questions to many supervisors in similar positions. These extracts from the records of a supervisor who worked with a social worker of limited capacity, highlights the supervisor's dilemma in providing a good client service with the means available.

It should be stated that although only one case has been singled out for discussion the concern here was also in relation to other cases and the general quality of work. The extracts demonstrate further, that greater skill is perhaps required when helping workers of more limited abilities; certainly greater ability to contain legitimate anxiety over the nature of the service given to the client is required.

This particular case was from the beginning bedevilled by a feeling that time was short, that unless appropriate help was offered at once the case was likely to deteriorate. This complicated case was handed to a worker who had never worked with adolescents, nor with delinquents; allocation took place before the arrival of this supervisor. This worker's previous function had been to befriend the elderly and to perform some concrete services. The supervisor, on the other hand, was very skilled in working with adolescents and found initial difficulty in fathoming this worker's ignorance about adolescence; she was also irritated by the worker's negatively critical attitude to this girl. The source of the worker's initial attitude was never really understood, though it did eventually undergo some change which made it possible to give some help to Betty.

Supervisors may also remember from their own personal experiences that it is not unusual to react negatively to some clients; the way to deal with this is to understand the reasons for it by getting the worker to share these with the supervisor, seeing the worker's picture without producing guilty feelings in the worker, feeding in appropriate knowledge, and by these means together with supervisor's patience and understanding to bring about a gradual change in attitude.

Although this supervisor made many strenuous attempts to help this worker, her main concern was for the fifteen-year-old girl in her predicament; this client's dilemma was uppermost in her mind and she became very intent to get the worker to understand the needs of this client. At one stage, one could almost sense the supervisor's wish to take over the care of this girl. With hindsight we can see that the pace of the worker was hastened beyond the latter's capacity.

One may now wonder whether the supervisor could have acknowledged the value of practical measures like finding other accommodation in the early stage and thereby allowed the worker to express her interest in the client in this form, perhaps the only way she was capable of doing at that time. These are questions not statements. Any supervisor in this position will be well aware of the complexities inherent in such a situation. In one sense this supervisor's extensive experience with teenagers might be said to have been a handicap. It is difficult for experienced workers to remember how differently they functioned at the beginning of their career with similar clients and before they had accumulated the knowledge and experience that they now possess. It was not till much later, really at the point when the worker's distressed state rendered the supervisor temporarily helpless too, that she rememberd how difficult teenagers can be and compared this difficult task with the social worker's previously more comfortable role. It would also have been helpful to assure the worker at a very early stage that many workers find teenagers difficult to work with.

Many of the points made relate to the supervisor's dual focus, the caring for the worker and the caring for the client. When the worker is of adequate capacity this is manageable; the difficulty arises when there exist serious questions about the worker's suitability to help clients. Let me repeat: the supervisor's primary function is to enable the worker to do better work. This requires a first assessment of the worker's level of functioning, which offers guidance as to normal difficulties in learning or idiosyncratic learning blocks relating to lack of knowledge or limitation in areas of feeling. The supervisor should always attempt to understand the reasons for poor functioning in certain areas.

This task was complicated because the worker had little learning opportunities but also seemed less able than others to draw on life experiences to help her understanding. The supervisor had cause to be concerned about her capacity to relate and her potential to develop.

This is an attempt to describe the complicated task that faces conscientious, concerned supervisors in social services departments who are interested in providing an adequate client service with inadequate resources. It raises the whole question of the minimum equipment a social worker requires and how client needs and social work equipment can be matched. In relation to the practice of supervision it has raised many questions which supervisors will wish to reflect on and relate to their own supervisory practice. It also demonstrates the supervisor's own pressure to teach perhaps too much, when it is apparent that too little is known by the worker to help the client adequately, but it also demonstrates that only so much can be absorbed by anyone.

This example is meant as a reflective exercise for supervisors. I am very grateful to this supervisor who so generously supplied the material.

5 Factors in learning and teaching

Adults as learners
To undertake sound comprehensive supervision the supervisor has to be equipped in two main areas: social work practice, and the field of adult learning. In this chapter, adult learning will be the main focus; only brief mention is given to competence in social work practice.

Equipment for social work practice includes knowledge and skill in the following areas:

> human growth and behaviour
> cultural factors
> the wider aspects of any given problem subject matter e.g. deprivation
> available agency and community resources
> the process of establishing a psycho-social diagnosis
> ways of evolving a feasible treatment plan
> interviewing techniques for flexible application with a wide range of clients.

She must not only possess theoretical knowledge in these areas but must understand how to apply it in practice.

Competence in social work practice includes insight into ways of operating; for example, understanding one's personal likes and dislikes, and how these affect the work if uncontrolled. Organizing ability, including the ordering of priorities in relation to the total work load and the timing of interrelated tasks, is also essential.

If supervision is to be a real opportunity for learning, the supervisor requires knowledge of the learning process. The main factors under consideration here are:

1 How adults learn and what creates a favourable climate: also what impedes development.
2 The early climate and how it affects learning attitudes far beyond childhood; learning patterns and attitudes, nature and origin.

3 Personality functioning in the learning process; the model of ego-psychology helps to explain what occurs during the process of learning.
4 The existence of ambivalence as a common phenomenon in learning together with the search for a comfortable equilibrium.
5 Motivation, capacity and opportunity will be reviewed.

The difference between what are normal, widely experienced factors in learning, and what are idiosyncratic factors will become apparent when the common stages in learning are discussed. Without this knowledge the supervisor is in danger of becoming confused, perceiving certain difficulties as belonging to the worker when in actual fact these are related to the common features of a particular stage of learning.

Early learning climate

It is useful to start at the beginning and consider the early learning pattern acquired during childhood. The parents create the initial climate in the home. The mother is the child's first teacher. The manner in which she enables the infant to do his learning greatly influences the formation of early attitudes to learning. (See Brodie and Axelrad's Film Series.) The degree of interest and the quality of enjoyment in her child and in his achievements, the readiness of her steady support when meeting new situations, will have considerable effect on his motivation to learn. The child who is being encouraged by the mother's joy and steady attention to experience new learning as his achievement and mastery, as 'I have done it', is learning by means of love, encouragement and hope. Most readers will have had the opportunity to observe a mother who has demonstrated her pleasure at the child's first step, heard her comment 'clever boy', and noted the child's response to repeat again and again what caused his mother's pleasure and approval. Such a child learns because of the mother, his relationship with her, and because of the favourable climate and opportunity she provides to explore, experiment and develop.

A less conducive climate will be created by a domineering mother (or father). The infant will not have a sense of achievement when mastering new skills, and learning is experienced as an enforcement. Because the child learns through fear or anger he tends to approach new situations in a timid, negative manner, and even when away from the original environment reacts in similar ways. He cannot discard easily his initial responses and tends to carry these with him into new situations. Feelings previously experienced in the home, especially in relation to the mother, become transferred into the new setting, for example the school. Confusion is likely to arise in the child's mind between the mother, his first teacher, and the new teacher at school. He will not readily recognize the helpful school teacher whose interest is solely in his development, but will regard her in the light of previous experience as a person to whom he may either have to submit, or whom he will have to fight like the new content she presents to him. This child will have gained little confidence in his ability to learn and to master new situations. His past experiences are affecting his responses. The experiences of a social worker are stated here to lend substance to this discussion; the illustrations will emphasize that many learning patterns are formed in the early years and are not easily discarded; also that learning patterns are the result of past experiences and personal idiosyncratic responses.

The learning climate in which this social worker and her brother found themselves as children was the same but each responded to it in a unique and personal way. She described vividly the way in which the authoritarian attitude of her father had affected her approach to new learning situations throughout her life. Her father, an intelligent but impatient man, had set high standards for his children. He expected them to know more than was usual for their age; he also expected them to think and act quickly. His curt manner and high expectations paralysed the little girl to the point of forgetting what she knew, and she found herself in a state where all she could do was to obey his instructions automatically; that is, without thinking. She recalls vividly one of the many instances. The whole family was in the car, the father driving; suddenly he stopped the car, thrust a letter at the child telling her to post it. Her immediate response was to put it into the letter-box nearest at hand. This turned out to be the letter-box of a bank, the post-box being a little further back. As on so many other occasions this led father to question in an irritated, exasperated way; 'You are not a fool, are you?' As she acted out of fear, thinking time was not available to her and so she found herself doing foolish things.

In school she worked hard to come up to expectations. When well prepared she could give the required answers but otherwise would remain silent as she dared not risk the wrong answers and appear foolish. Later, as a social work student she was hesitant and tentative, again not risking to make firm statements. She found herself unable to put pertinent questions to the psychiatric registrar, a fellow learner, when she had every reason to doubt the correctness of the diagnosis and subsequent treatment plan affecting the clients with whom she was to be working, and for whom she had much concern. The anxiety experienced in new situations when a child, where the father had set a chilly climate, could not easily be thrown off. Not until she entered social work training did she get insight into her behaviour. Even now, years later, she can still experience undue anxiety in a learning situation. She considers that as a result of this progress is slower than it would otherwise be.

The social worker's brother responded with anger rather than anxiety to this severe learning climate at home. Feeling under attack as a boy, he refused to learn at home and in school. He was a puzzle to his teachers who considered him intelligent, yet he made only slow progress. The sister sees him as having been in continuous conflict, wishing to learn and exercise his undoubted intelligence yet not allowing anyone to teach him because this had come to mean submission to his father. It took him longer than usual to gain qualification in his profession. He wanted to learn, to achieve, yet struggled in order not to succumb to the aspirations of his father. Even now, as a grown man, he will resist in situations that make him feel that he is being told what to do, to the point of refusing to read written instructions which would enable him to carry through a particular task that he wishes to master.

These examples underline the impact of early relationships and early learning climate on later attitudes to learning. Throughout childhood and adolescence other significant people influence attitudes to learning and either reinforce earlier patterns or bring about a certain measure of modification. The reader may well wish to reflect on his own attitude to learning and ponder the reasons for his particular mode.

The ambivalent element in learning
The strongest human motive is the urge to survive, with comfort if possible. In our society not many people have to struggle to keep physically alive. However, in most people's life there comes a stage when effort has to be made for emotional survival. In times of crisis the struggle to survive becomes very evident. Only when basic survival needs have been met is surplus energy available for learning, i.e. for acquiring further knowledge and skills, and for the achievement of ambitions.

Adults, whether social work students or qualified social workers, bring with them a personal life style which reflects their adaptation to environmental circumstances and inner needs; a pattern which has so far made for personal survival. To alter this pattern requires a major effort. Yet learning in social work requires modification or change of some of these life patterns, since this learning affects not only the areas of thinking but those of feeling and doing, hence of being.

Learning provides a challenge. There are moments of excitement and joy when discovering new knowledge and when hopeful of doing better work. These are the positive, the promise experiences. Learning something new and putting it to use, however, necessitates also the reviewing and scrutinising of previous knowledge and past practice, leading to serious stocktaking of what has been useful, but also of what has been nonfunctional, what needs preserving and what needs discarding.

Unlearning (or discarding) what has been part of a person's thinking and actions at a point when the newly acquired knowledge is not yet ripe for use, means entering into a phase of uncertainty. The adult learner cannot be sure any longer of the usefulness of earlier knowledge and practice, yet there also exists doubt whether what has just been acquired can be used. The learner thus finds himself in an unfamiliar territory of not knowing. The previous balance has been upset and this causes discomfort, tension, and raises feelings of anxiety and precariousness. Until a new balance can be established, the learner is suspended and is so to speak in limbo. He cannot be sure how he will fare and how he will come out of this.

Fear for survival is very much in the forefront of the mind of students at all levels of social work learning, and is reflected in questions like 'What will this do to me? Will it change me?' 'I want to learn more but do not want to change too much.' 'Can I survive and be comfortable again?' These are important considerations. Some people find it hard to take this risk. Being exposed to new learning experiences and new situations means giving up, at least for a time, the comfortable feeling of knowing what to do. The state of unease brought about by the new will remain until either the personality has been able to incorporate and make use of it, or has warded it off, as a means of survival. The supervisor can do much to facilitate and encourage the promise experiences by creating a conducive climate, whilst knowing at the same time that some of the energy will also be channelled into protecting the self. To sum up, the wish to learn more has a counterpart in the need to stay the same. On the one hand, there is a search for knowledge in the hope that this will bring about greater understanding and ease, leading to greater adequacy and job satisfaction; and on the other hand, a fear of what this new knowledge will do to the self.

Personality functioning in learning

The model of ego-psychology can help us to understand what takes place in the learning process. Ego-psychology puts emphasis on the functioning of the ego and therefore is concerned with that part of the personality that is most in touch with reality. As the reader will know, the psycho-analytic system of personality functioning has three sub-systems: the Id, largely concerned with instinctual life and primitive pleasure; the superego or conscience, the standard setter; and the ego, that part of the personality which deals with seeing, hearing, knowing and receiving stimuli from outside as well as from inside. It is the ego that has to do most of the work when it comes to learning. The function of the ego can be said to have a three-fold task:

1. to *perceive* inner need and outer reality and to mediate between the two to find a satisfactory solution;
2. to *integrate* the personal needs with the social demands, the old familiar ones with the new unfamiliar ones;
3. to *protect* the personality from too great a pressure from without or from within and so to ensure survival by using various mechanisms of defence.

When all goes well, and the amount of new content is not too massive, the tempo towards change is not too rapid and the nature of the 'new' does not constitute too great a threat to the personality, the integrative function comes into operation when the personality begins to adapt and make use of the change. When, on the other hand, too much change is occurring too quickly and the 'new' cannot be accommodated by the personality, the protective function of the ego has to operate. This protective mechanism demonstrates the personality's inability or resistance to absorb the new. 'Too much', relates to the quantity and the quality of the 'new'; either can make the individual feel under extreme threat. When this occurs the integrative mechanism of the ego ceases to function and the protective mechanism comes into play. Instead of the ego absorbing the new and being able to deal with change, the protective mechanism wards off what cannot be absorbed, and so safeguards the personality from what it cannot take. This mechanism exists for the purpose of protecting the personality from becoming overwhelmed or completely disorganized.

The recent reorganizations of the social services (1971 and 1974) have provided us with first-hand evidence of what happens when too many changes occur too quickly, and the effect on social workers and social work. Many staff were driven to defend 'the self' against the onslaught of the massive 'new' which could not be accommodated. The defence frequently took the form of not seeing, not hearing, even not feeling and at times not speaking. Communication, one of the most vital social work tools, was thus affected outside the department with clients and inside the department with staff and colleagues.

Defending is done in a variety of ways. As stated already, not seeing, not hearing, not communicating, are common means. Other phenomena are non-thinking or developing stereo-type thinking; becoming dependent and regressing to earlier, more satisfying levels; and projecting.

Stereotype thinking means that constructive thinking is abandoned. For example, following the Curtis Report the tendency towards the automatic boarding out of children without careful assessment of the readiness of a particular child demonstrated one such stereotype, while in the present post-Seebohm era a too literal interpretation of the report has resulted in yet another stereotype, 'one family one worker', frequently leading to obliterating exploratory, constructive thinking in relation to the needs of individual families.

Regression, another mechanism of defence, is expressed by moving away from present functioning and reverting to an earlier level when more comfort and satisfaction was experienced. It is another way of attempting to deal with too much new input. The example of the student, formerly a clerk, who removed himself from the social work task by claiming that none of his clients needed help, and instead placed himself in the clerical section with former colleagues where he felt of use, illustrates this point. A further example is the tutor who spends much of his time acting as supervisor rather than undertaking tutorial functions. This can be an indication that the tutor is not comfortable in his new role and is reverting to an earlier one which provided him with greater satisfaction. The excuse that the poor quality of supervision makes this role switch necessary is not convincing since other means can be employed towards improving supervisory practice. Similar examples will come to mind that the reader may wish to consider.

Projection, another mechanism of defence, takes the form 'This is nothing to do with me – I am all right!' It is all to do with others; it is to do with the supervisor, the hierarchy or those people at headquarters. (I am not suggesting that this can never be reality!) The aim here, however, is to draw attention to this mechanism which becomes more operative when people are under stress.

The supervisor who encounters these defences should recognize them for what they are; a signal that the worker cannot take in any more. There is no point in teaching when no learning can take place, nor in introducing new tasks when these cannot be tackled with some degree of confidence and adequacy. There is no sense in introducing yet another type of client when the worker's signal indicates that he can barely cope with the current allocation. The supervisor must continually ask herself 'What is this worker's capacity, am I asking more of him than he is capable of? Am I putting him into too many situations too quickly?' She should also ask herself, 'Am I giving him enough support during this period of learning?' for this too will affect his capacity to integrate the new. When a social worker has to carry unsupported too much stress and strain, the warding-off mechanism comes into operation. In the case of a hospital social worker this was demonstrated by the way she discussed in a flat disinterested manner, lacking all feeling, the traumatic experiences of the patients. By recounting the severe injuries, disfigurements, amputations of patients with this marked lack of concern, she could deny their suffering. This she could not face by herself and there were no ready opportunities to share her feelings within the hospital setting; her only way of dealing with the distress of others was by denying that it existed. This served as her protection.

There are many examples of members of the caring professions who cannot do the necessary caring because of lack of adequate support. Have you wondered sometimes why the nurse in a residential nursery so often deals with a number of children and whether this is to avoid the pain that comes when facing the massive distress of one little child? Have you sometimes questioned why so many social workers take on far too many cases? Is there hidden hope that by fragmenting the work to the point of ineffectiveness a great deal of personal pain can be avoided? These are important considerations, and special knowledge and understanding are required to establish helpful supervision. Some fundamental principles are therefore listed:

1 The supervisor has to have understanding of how much new knowledge can be absorbed by anyone at any one time and what variety of cases can be adequately managed by a beginning social worker. Some supervisors feel a need to supply knowledge irrespective of whether the social worker can use it. The importance lies always in what is *learned* rather than what is taught.
2 The supervisor will have to take note of the quality and the structure of the worker's ego. This will give an indication of how much 'new' can be integrated by this social worker. The supervisor must recognize and be sensitive to the worker's attempt to ward off what is too much. Some social workers can absorb more than others. Some personality structures are more elastic and therefore can accommodate more than others. The supervisor should ensure as far as possible that the integrative function of the ego is in operation rather than the protective, warding-off function. The example of a newly qualified worker who has been in a post for three months is fairly typical:

> When confronted with another complex case this social worker explained that he could help the family with the practical housing

issue but could not help with regard to their marital problem. For this he wanted to refer them to marriage guidance. The supervisor was perplexed by what at first seemed a strange division of work. Exploration with the worker, however, revealed that he had had too much to cope with in these three short months. He had been confronted with a great mixture of cases: guardian *ad litem*, a number of care orders, a family's predicament over the mother's suffering from multiple sclerosis; he had also to assess a case of potential battering, as well as dealing with the admission of an old lady to a Home. A relevant lecture here and there while on the course was no preparation for this complex caseload. It was hardly surprising that he felt bewildered and confused by the many new tasks and problems he was presented with in such a short span of time. One could only feel thankful that he had a built-in protective mechanism that by its operation preserved him from complete inner chaos. One could also be thankful that he had a supervisor sensitive enough to explore this situation with him, and who realized, if only eventually, that her expectations had been totally unrealistic.

3 The supervisor needs to understand that the learner requires support during the period of learning. Learning can best take place in a supportive climate. Not many people are able to learn under threat and in the absence of necessary support.

Climate for learning
Bertha Reynolds (1942) comments, 'Growth is natural to all living things, the way to enable this is to study the process of growth and cooperate with it by nourishing the soil and pulling out the weeds.' In other words, to facilitate good learning conditions and to recognize the individual mode of learning.

All supervisors need to reflect on what is a favourable climate; how does one set about creating it, for example, for a new social worker? The following considerations may aid supervisors' thinking:

A new social worker comes from a familiar setting to an unfamiliar one. He may come from the protective setting of a social work course or from another social work agency. In either case, he comes from a familiar setting where he knew his tasks, his responsibilities, where he was a recognised member of a work group, to a new department where initially he has none of these certainties. Many aspects of the agency will be new; he will not know the practices and expectations of the department; he has moved from a position of knowing where he was to one of not being sure where he is. This will make for initial anxiety, dependency, and doubts about his usefulness. How, then, does the supervisor create the opportunity for him to work and learn productively?

The supervisor can, in the first place, help by stressing what is familiar in the unfamiliar, and by demonstrating that the worker's previous experiences have relevance in the new setting. The following example will illuminate this particular aspect:

> This new worker had come from a somewhat unstructured, unorthodox social work setting, into a structured one. He felt unsure whether the experience he had had in the previous setting would be useful and acceptable in the new work sphere. As one of his first clients, he had to deal with a mother who very much regretted the parting of her own worker and felt reluctant to change to a new one. She had made this quite explicit to her previous worker, but since she required more help, and since the old worker was leaving, had grudgingly agreed to the transfer.
> On seeing the new worker, the woman responded by explaining that she did not wish to see him; she had just had a tooth out, therefore she was unable to speak. She did not look at the new worker while saying this and remained seated. The new worker sympathised and agreed that it would not be easy for her to talk; he thought he would make her a cup of tea and they could just sit and drink this together; and so it happened. The woman relaxed and they drank their tea in companionable silence. After a while she asked for the worker's name, saying 'I can take it in now!'

From the woman's response the worker could, in fact, have known that he had found an appropriate way of making contact with this client. However, this in itself was not sufficient for this new worker. At this early stage it was important for the supervisor to acknowledge that the skills acquired in his former setting were relevant and useful in the present one, and that his empathic understanding for people would be a major aid in social work. At that stage of realistic dependency, the acceptance of the worker's contribution by the supervisor, and the latter's realistic reassurance, is most important. Even a few months later this worker no longer required this; he again knew what he could do.

Charlotte Towle (1954) discusses different kinds of dependency: realistic dependency results from the feelings engendered during the initial phase, mainly created by lack of knowledge and understanding to meet with confidence the demands of the job; emotional dependency has a broader origin and includes realistic inadequacy, but puts more emphasis on the psychological effect of enforced change, the possible activation of earlier conflict, and the meaning to the learner of having others dependent upon him when he himself feels dependent. The initial phase of realistic dependency can be shortened by the supervisor giving security and order. This she can do by being readily available to deal with pressing questions and concerns and not to keep him waiting until the next supervisory session. The latter practice increases, quite unnecessarily, feelings of precariousness and discomfort. Most learners do not stay long in this phase but are encouraged by the supervisor's acknowledgement of work 'well done' as seen in the above illustration. By establishing a link between the learner's previous practice and current practice, some feelings of the unfamiliar can be dispelled and some confidence regained.

The following illustration (Cleugh, 1962) describes the behaviour of two adults, each struggling with a new learning situation. It can be assumed that each of them is attempting to cope with feelings of realistic dependency but neither receives the necessary support. It is quoted here because this is not an uncommon situation in social work.

(For Mr Humber read 'supervisor', for Miss E read 'social worker'.)

> Mr Humber was new to the work of tutoring adults, his previous experience having been with post-graduates in the university department of education. He found working with grown-ups rather a strain, because they were 'so opinionated.' The older ones particularly 'thought they knew it all because they had been doing it some time' and 'were not ready to learn.' 'They tried to tell me' and 'they argue', were other complaints. To deal with the situation he had given the chief trouble-maker, Miss E, who was older than he was, a practical assignment in a particularly tough area, in the hope that this would make her more conscious of her deficiencies and so ready to accept guidance. In conversation, Mr Humber gave the impression of having a rather punitive attitude towards this woman, who was frustrating his efforts to bring the blessings of modern knowledge to her and who preferred to remain in her own primitive state ...
>
> On the other side, we have a middle-aged woman who has removed herself from her familiar environment where she was successful according to her lights, and entered an unfamiliar and exacting milieu where she may or may not make good. On any showing that requires some courage and the less her ability the more courage it needs. Only a very insensitive person could fail to feel uncertain. In such a situation some will make a bid for sympathy and support and, by proclaiming their dependence, hope to enlist the aid of authority. Others will parade their competence, maybe rather

aggressively as Miss E did, but feel nontheless unsure. On the other side, we have a tutor in his first year, keen, hardworking, enthusiastic, anxious to make a success of his new job and rather conscious that he is working by himself. He, too, has removed himself from his familiar environment where he was successful, and so on ... to avoid repetition.

Many a supervisor may at times have behaved similarly to Mr Humber or felt like doing so. When a supervisor is new to the task of supervising, is as yet uncertain of the role and is also unsure of the supervisory contribution she can make, acknowledgement and approval from the supervisee is asked for in the absence of more appropriate support. The supervisee in these circumstances also unsupported, has to protect himself. Neither supervisor nor social worker can develop. The climate is unsuitable. Under these circumstances the supervisor tends to regard challenging questions by the social worker as an attack on herself and therefore may well be unable to see how these relate to the uncertainty of the learner and his struggle. This kind of situation is likely to occur when a supervisor is left to struggle alone with the new taks, as is frequently the case in a social services department.

If Mr Humber had had available a supervisor or a consultant with whom he could have discussed his experiences and feelings of uncertainty, he would probably have been able to deal with Miss E in a far more constructive way. As he had, however, to struggle on his own with this new task, he had to direct much of his attention and energy towards the self, instead of directing it towards the other person, the explicit learner. This is an example of a poor learning climate; the unprepared, unsupported teacher could do no better.

What, then, is a favourable climate for the beginning social worker to learn and function? How much time does he require to settle in and find his feet? Reynolds (1942) believes in getting the newcomer quickly into operation and finding his own way of helping people: 'This is as fundamental as placing the voice in singing, or learning the correct bodily balance in dancing.' It will help him to focus on his work, rather than too exclusively on himself. It is necessary to make some assessment of the capacity of the new worker, so that he can be given work that corresponds with what he can do. He should experience early on that he is useful and needed. Everyone needs to feel of use, especially the beginning worker. Children frequently build up a picture of the sort of people they are from the behaviour and comments of people around them. Adults in new situations are similarly dependent on those around them and require realistic reassurance of their contributions. The newcomer is vulnerable;

he is not yet part of a group, is unsure of his position and cannot know how he will be regarded. Teams and supervisors, on the other hand, have their own fears and apprehensions about newcomers; will he disrupt what exists, upset the balance and be a challenge? Expectation of his contribution may be quite unrealistic and relate more to the hopes or fears of workers rather than the newcomer's capacity.

At the beginning the worker will ask more questions, some will seem essential, others unnecessary. The supervisor's response to these is important. If the supervisor responds defensively, the effect on the worker's attitude to questioning and exploration may be longlasting. The supervisor who encourages questioning also encourages critical thinking and the examination of situations; thus she not only encourages the worker to understand the present situation, but strengthens for all times the newcomer's critical thinking, a very necessary social work tool. Questioning, exploring and comprehending are part and parcel of social work practice. Without these there can be no real understanding, whether in relation to helping clients or evaluating old practices and new methods.

The need to provide factual information required by the worker to carry out his new tasks cannot be overstressed. Without this he cannot be expected to function. He requires an overall picture of the organization and where he fits into the structure; information as to who the key figures and the resource people are whose assistance he may require in the future. He needs to be put into the picture about how communication takes place in this organization, and made to feel welcome not only by sincere comment but by such practical demonstration as the readiness of his own room with desk, chair and armchairs for interviewing, and all the other necessary equipment for starting work. It is essential that he has a place to call his own so that he has the opportunity to start to work constructively. Many readers will unfortunately be reminded of their own feelings of discouragement and despondency when on arrival they had none of these essential work facilities and had to make it their first effort to obtain a work diary, a pen and paper to write! The supervisor should set aside enough time to introduce the new worker into the essentials and to see that other colleagues are also available to him. A welcoming team is a great support to a new worker. It is generally helpful, even at this early stage, to have some clarification of mutual expectations so that the new worker can have a realistic idea of what will be expected of him. When a plan exists, for example, for regular supervisory sessions, it is helpful to inform the worker of this rather than to leave him wondering. Agency manuals relating to policy and practice can sometimes provide a valuable addition to the other means of orientation. Everything should be done to help the worker pass through this unfamiliar stage and to aid him in acquiring more certainty of his own role and function. The initial climate in which the new worker finds himself is exceedingly important and lays the foundation for the good work to follow.

Common stages in learning

Miss Reynolds' clear description of the stages of learning in *Learning and Teaching in the Practice of Social Work* needs no further elaboration. The importance of her contribution is her detailed description of what is common in learning. It is important in social work to take account of what are normal developmental phenomena especially as social work is problem centred. The description of the stages of learning enables us to be more accurate in our assessment of what is a normal common stage of learning and what is related to the individual way a particular social worker does his learning. Miss Reynolds has highlighted the complexity in social work learning; she has clarified that the possession of knowledge does not automatically mean that this is then available for use because of the inevitable lag between acquiring knowledge and the developing ability to apply this knowledge in practice. She has made it clear that only by understanding what is common to all learners can the supervisor hope to identify the learning pattern of the individual learner.

Although Miss Reynolds has developed her material mainly from her teaching of social work students, the common stages in learning are equally relevant to social workers at all levels and have special meaning for the newly qualified social worker. Social work practitioners, no matter how experienced, will always continue to learn and to discover new facets to their work. Hence the stages of learning are applicable throughout a social worker's professional life. Miss Reynolds writes:

> In the teaching and learning of a profession like social work, which involves meeting many experiences which are new, there are distinguished five stages of the use of conscious attention, related to the safety of the person as well as to the goal of mastery of the experience. One should not expect to see a learner pass through these stages in well-marked order,* for no one can take one new experience at a time and see it through. Such a person is constantly using old learnings to master new details, and he can never have done with the need to go back to early stages with each new portion of the whole experience which threatens his security. Progress from one stage to another, however (in a process which is as well understood as is the practice of an art), should be discernible in general, despite many regressions in detail. A knowledge of what these stages are is indispensable to one who is guiding a learning

process in any of the arts, for without some such directive, regressions may seem willful, or evidence of hopeless incapacity; stimulation of conscious awareness may be given at precisely the times when it throws the learner back into self-conscious inability to relate himself normally to the situation. If a teacher can be guided by what is happening to the learner, rather than by what he himself wants to accomplish by means of the learner, he will be in a position really to teach what he has to give. We shall return to this theme with many illustrations in later sections. For the present, let us look at the stages of use of conscious intelligence as learning progresses.

---

*Throughout this whole discussion, and in reference to later chapters to these stages of the use of conscious attention (or intelligence), it should be borne in mind that these stages are, for the reason just given, never well marked and absolute. Like the passage from childhood to adolescence and and from youth to adulthood, there are no distinct boundaries, and reversions are frequent. Yet, in general, in dealing with a certain kind of behaviour in a person it makes a difference whether he is a child, an adolescent, or an adult. The plea throughout our discussion is to be clear enough about development not to treat children (in this experience of social work) like adults or adults like children.

I   THE STAGE OF ACUTE CONSCIOUSNESS OF SELF
It may seem like a contradiction in terms to call this a stage of learning. It feels to the victim as if he had no intelligence, to say nothing of using it. Yet, as we have seen, it is a step in advance of being limited to what automatic responses can do, and the distress is a signal that danger to the person may be present and energies must be mobilized. One could wish that attention need not be fixed on the self in so paralyzing a manner, but to forget to preserve one's life would be a biological tragedy. Practically, the period of inability to act is comparatively short, and energies are rallied which call out responses in which the person has some security.

Stage fright is a classic example. People who report the agony of going back almost to zero in their tongue-tied emptiness of resource say that what pulls them out of it is the beginning to use some well-acquired coordination like walking. Sometimes they open their mouths fully expecting that nothing will come, but their success in saying something frees them to go on. It may be a fear greater than the fear of the sea of faces that energizes them for self-preservation ('I must not fail and disgrace myself'), or anger at their own helplessness gives them strength. In an emergency people do what is most characteristic of them. Some keep as still as possible; some talk volubly, or make 'wise-cracks'; some become aggressive lest anyone know how scared they are. (These can be psychic substitutes for flight.) A teacher can recognize varying symptoms of insecurity for what they are. It is not necessary to label the person as being such and such a sort if the teacher remembers that everyone reverts to some earlier pattern when he is sufficiently threatened by a new situation. Above all, it is desirable that the teacher be not in turn threatened by this behaviour to the point of punishing the learner for the teacher's insecurity. The role of the teacher in this stage of learning is security-giving, helping the learner to find the solid ground of personal adequacy he already has on which to plant his feet while he struggles with the new experience.

II THE STAGE OF SINK-OR-SWIM ADAPTATION

How does anyone ever get out of the first stage of acute self-consciousness? He receives enough energy from his physiological adaptation to a fearsome situation, and from his initiation, of some activity in which he is relatively secure, to take at least partial note of his surroundings. This may be only with the margin of his consciousness while the focus of it is still upon himself, and on the biological problem of whether to save his life best by advance or retreat. As the eye of the motorist sees a signal from the environment to get into emergency action, even though his attention has been occupied elsewhere, so the learner, bewildered though he may be, catches hold of something in the situation to which he can respond. He gets an inkling of what people want of him, even though his preoccupation with himself makes him partially insensitive. If he hits upon a response which others react to favourably, he is encouraged to go on. Like a poor swimmer falling into the water, he may have little sense of where the wharf is or how to get there, but he may succeed in keeping afloat at least, till he knows where he is and can save himself or be rescued. This second stage of barely keeping up with what the situation demands from moment to moment may last a long time, and is apt to be a period of dependence upon approval or disapproval from people who are seemingly at home in the situation. It is a deceptive period for those who guide the experience, particularly if one of the ways of responding to guidance is the acquisition of a vocabulary which makes the learner sound as if he had mastered the whole science and art of the new activity, when his performance reveals just the contrary is true. It is hard to be patient with a person who talks so well and does so poorly. Again, the teacher's own automatic responses get in the way. It is hard to remember that skills which are now so much a part of oneself that there is no need to think of them were once as hard to practise as the student finds them now. It is essential to remember, however, that at this stage the learner cannot understand the meaning of what he is doing as he will later. One may attempt to make him more conscious of what he is about than his present adjustment to the experience will let him be, but these attempts only increase his confusion and throw him back to a still greater sense of an overwhelming newness which he fears he can never master. Skilled teaching, at this stage, carries on the function of increasing security through mobilizing the knowledge and skills the learner already has, and encouraging him to trust and use his 'spontaneous' responses. The term may be misleading, for it does not represent accidental, 'out-of-the-blue' activity, but the use the student makes of what has already become a part of him. These coordinations of energy which are characteristic of the person may not be the best adapted to the art which is being learned, but their correction can come about after they have been expressed and when the person is more ready to give them up than he can be at this stage when he needs everything which is his own. Criticism applied before the teacher knows what the person's patterns of behaviour are, and how much they need to be modified to suit the new situation, can only do harm. During this stage the best skill of the teacher is required to free the learner from his fears and the rigidities acquired in his childhood reactions to a not-always wise discipline. This is not done by a pseudo-psychotherapeutic method, but by using the daily business of class discussion or field practice to create an atmosphere of relaxed yet stimulating activity. Once the learner can be himself in the new situation, he can be helped to change as much as he will have to change to adapt to what the situation will demand of him, or to seek some other field of work.

If this stage of learning seems to be a predominantly protected one, while the learner is finding himself and beginning to trust the authority of the experienced person who will later help him to be self-critical, it is also a period when there should be some stimulation. We have all seen beginners too easily satisfied with their first superficial adjustments to want to go on with the pain of struggling with difficulties. The relationship to the teacher can be made stimulating, as well as protective, if it gives some picture of what fine accomplishment is, along with reassurance that one is not expected to reach it immediately.

III THE STAGE OF UNDERSTANDING THE SITUATION WITHOUT POWER TO CONTROL ONE'S OWN ACTIVITY IN IT

Again, progress from one stage (the second) to another (the third) is a concomitant of release of energy from preoccupation with the self to freedom to study the situation as it is. The suddenness with which comprehension seems to come is a matter of surprise to learners and teachers alike. Whether it is the art of swimming, or piano playing or social work, the learner says something like this: 'All at once it came to me. I thought I knew before what it was all about, but now I know I have been in a fog all this time,' or 'it was all words to me, and now it has come alive.' Although we may explain these sudden illuminations as the end of a long period of adjustment to new concepts and skills, a period in which the unconscious reorganization plays an important part, there is much about this phenomenon that invariably seems miraculous.

In practice, the learner has a severe hazard to overcome very soon. He thinks he has mastered the art, and finds the practice of what he understands so well still lagging behind. Why? Conscious intelligence is now able to deal with the new situation, but conscious intelligence is never enough. The learner has been using more or less automatic responses all during the period when he did not understand what he was doing, and he must use them still until the new ways of working which are consciously being mastered have become a part of himself. He has as yet no base of stabilized responses built up for this situation, on which he can rely while learning constantly new details. He understands what should be done, but is very uneven in his ability to do it.

Here the teacher can easily be destructive. It seems absurd that one who admits now that he understands should perform most of the time on so low a level. If months have elapsed in reaching this stage, it looks as if the supervisor had failed when a learner does so poorly. It is hard to avoid thinking: 'He can do better if he wants to. He did better last week.' One is tempted to use criticism more in retaliation for the supervisor's frustration than for its teaching value. If the supervisor understands, however, the psychological inevitability of this stage, and can give reassurance that everyone goes through this experience, there is now an opportunity to enlist the intelligence of the learner as never before, and criticism can now be at its optimum helpfulness. The learner can now, with help, think out for himself, after his spontaneous responses have apparently failed him, why they are inadequate, and how his intellectual appreciation of what the situation demands can be turned to use in later trials of his skill. One can help a learner to say, without loss of courage: 'I made a mess of that, didn't I? But now I understand where I didn't quite get hold, and I'm anxious to see if I can't better that point next time'. Partial successes can be emphasized to overcome the tendency of all beginners to regard every small slip as evidence of total incapacity. The third stage may last a long time, perhaps for years, before a worker can be said to be living most of his time in Stage IV, if indeed he ever reaches it. Our whole field of social work is only partially able, even now, to claim a clear understanding of what it is we are doing, to say nothing of being able to do as well as we know. It is not to be expected, then, that students will reach in any period of training and early practice, a mastery which not many of the most skilled people in the field have yet reached. We see enough, however, to map out for our further progress the following two stages, and a supervisor needs to know the road ahead, even though it is still to be experienced in its full achievement.

IV THE STAGE OF RELATIVE MASTERY, IN WHICH ONE CAN BOTH UNDERSTAND AND CONTROL ONE'S OWN ACTIVITY IN THE ART WHICH IS LEARNED

Now what was new in the experience has really become a part of the person. He does not have to think of himself, out of fear of what the experience will do to him. He knows he can deal with it and why, because he understands what it is, and what its demands will be. He has related its new skills to his old acquired skills and to his natural emotional responses to situations. Conscious intelligence and unconscious responses are working together in an integrated wholeness of functioning. So much of the activity as is routine is taken care of with minimum expenditure of energy, leaving conscious attention to the study of new aspects of the activity as they arise in contact with the environment. The person can think of himself now in a new way – objectively. He can see himself working as he might see another person in the situation working. He can criticize and change his approach as the situation demands something different. He has become professional in that he can apply knowledge to the solving of practical problems, using himself as instrument, with all his acquired skills and his emotional responses disciplined and integrated to the professional purpose.

When this stage is reached is there any need for a teacher or supervisor? One who has come thus far may be expected to be his own supervisor to a large extent. Yet this period has its peculiar dangers, as does every other. For the comparatively few who reach this level of competence, the temptation is great to feel 'finished'. Without the stimulus of much competition and in a position of leadership, it is easy to forget that situations never repeat themselves, and there is always something new to be mastered. It is easy to become smug, and use in a stereotyped way skills which were mastered with so sensitive an awareness. The tragedy of this is not only in the arteriosclerosis of the person's own work, but in the need he has to protect himself against the growth of younger people. They see new things constantly, and challenge the comfort of accustomed ways. The leader does not want to go back to the early stages of learning, as he must if he is to be in touch with the new aspects of the changing situation and, unconsciously or consciously, he has need to force learners not to disturb him with their growth. As one executive said: 'We have spent years learning how to run this agency, and do you think we can let a new worker upset all that, trying experiments we have long ago discarded?'

Professional people and artists find that they need stimulation to learn always. Usually it has to come from their colleagues in informal consultation, with the seeking of experts to advise in special problems. A research interest is essential if one is not to go stale. Contact with studies in related fields and observing the practice of other arts are fine antidotes for a narrowing interest. It is only comparative mastery that can be attained in any field, and what is mastery today is apprenticeship tomorrow.

V THE STAGE OF LEARNING TO TEACH WHAT ONE HAS MASTERED

There is a prevailing idea that what one knows one can *ipso facto* teach. That idea comes from a subject-centred concept of education. When education is oriented to the person who is to learn plus the situation to be mastered, there is something more to teaching than proving to the learner that one knows the subject. Can we think of progression from Stage IV to Stage V in the same terms as earlier transitions, that is, in terms of release of energy from one focus of attention to freedom to take on another? Although PART V will discuss this in more detail, we note here that we can expect a similar release of energy, which is now freed from preoccupation with subject matter, to an ability to understand the difficulties of the person who is learning. The teacher is now free enough to be able to see how each learner works best, what motivations favour learning and what ones need to be outgrown by a particular individual, what phases of the subject are obscure and what are clear already and can be used for building up security, at what point help is needed and when it is in the way.

There will be times when the teacher is himself in Stage II and does not know what he is doing to help but hopes students will learn somehow. There are discouraging periods after he has been thrilled by the idea that he knows how to teach when he cannot do as well as he knows and berates himself for the stupid destructive things he has done (Stage III). These stages are repeated, not once but many times, as ever-new problems present themselves. The teacher needs as much as any student the guidance of a supervisor of his teaching who can give him the encouragement of a relationship to someone who sees the whole process in larger perspective. Until he reaches the stage of comparative mastery of teaching (IV), or that of teaching other teachers of social work (V), the teacher may feel the deprivation of some of the satisfaction of his own practice of his art. It is to be hoped that no teacher of social work is required to give up all practice so completely that teaching becomes the dried husk of the past. A teacher is at his best when he is learning best, in close touch with his material and with each successive student whose learning constitutes an ever-new challenge. He can then glory in the successes of others as once he gloried in his own.

The preceding account of the stages of use of conscious intelligence in learning forms only the background for the work with individual learners which the teacher carries on in class groups or in supervision of field practice. There is probably no way in which persons show their distinctively individual characteristics more than in their reactions to a learning situation. Some withdraw and can be taught only in a pursuit of themselves which is both fear-relieving and enticing. Some are challenged by difficulties and others repelled. Some are filled with curiosity and others ask only to be left alone with what is familiar. The differences are not simple, as these examples may suggest, but extremely complex, involving the whole personality. We shall study in PART III and PART IV the ways in which a teacher or supervisor tries to reach an educational diagnosis which will be a guide to understanding how students learn best and how they may be helped. It is not only that the teacher brings his intelligence to supplement that of the learners, but it is necessary to release theirs to its most complete use, through understanding of their individual differences and of the motivations which are most effective with them.

There is another aspect of learning which a teacher should not lose sight of – the influence of the culture in which people live upon their capacity to learn and the kinds of learning they can assimilate. The writer has found, for example, a distinct difference in the way [American] students from the South approach learning social work,

69

as compared with those from the North and East or the Middle Western states. All of these regional differences merge, more or less, in the competitive urban culture which surrounds most of the centres for field training of schools of social work, but some students have to make more adjustments than others in order to achieve the qualities which this culture seems to demand and almost automatically to select. To study learners to see what they bring to the learning experience and how they change in it, as a group as well as individually in contact with the social forces playing upon them, calls for all the conscious intelligence we have as teachers and supervisors of field practice.

Linked to the stages of learning is the learning rhythm, the movement that occurs throughout the different learning stages. Most learners take hold of the new content, become interested in it for a time, then lose interest. At some later point they again become engaged, take hold again of the new content and gradually find that it can be used in practice. This rhythm, taking in, moving on, then standing still before a further move towards consolidation takes place, is usual. Supervisors need to know that these are regular phenomena and recognize that the learning process consists of forward movements but also of plateaux and halts. The latter do not indicate individual shortcomings or resistances but are common and necessary aids towards constructive learning. Within this common rhythm there are of course individual nuances. Learning blocks have to be recognised and understood before they can be worked through. Only if very severe may these signify unsuitability for social work. Because social work is problem centred and social workers are concerned with poor, unhealthy functioning of their clients, supervisors have to guard against focussing too readily on the poor functioning of a worker and mistake for problematic what in essence are common healthy features towards further learning and survival.

Individual learning patterns
While stages and rhythm relate to what is common in learning, patterns relate to what is individual. The supervisor needs to understand the way in which a particular worker does his learning, so that a way of teaching best suited to him can be found. The supervisor also needs to know that only a certain amount of knowledge can be digested at any one time and take note of what is manageable for a particular worker.

Reactions to learning are varied and include a range of feelings, from excitement, challenge and joy at new discoveries, to threat and fear of defeat. These attitudes are linked with past experiences. The more success there has been in learning, the greater is the hope of achievement and the less the fear of failure. The supervisor needs to be aware how these attitudes affect the learning pace. There are many different individual learning patterns. The reader may wish to reflect on his own particular pattern of learning and on the method of teaching, that has over the years been most helpful and acceptable to him.

Some learners can begin to learn and function best when they can see others operate; in this way they are offered in the early stages the opportunity of learning by example, even though later they will want to make their own adaptation and develop their own style. This way of learning means that security is gained by seeing someone else act in a situation before the worker risks his own self. It is learning by doing but the 'doing' is undertaken by someone else and this is used as preparation. It is particularly helpful when the senior person in this situation is also liked and respected. One might call this the 'apprenticeship method. It is not often used nowadays by design and has gone out of fashion, except in the field of community work, where the nature and operation of the work frequently requires the use of this model.

Some learners find it helpful to discuss beforehand the situation in which they are likely to find themselves but rely on being told how the supervisor would tackle that task. Supervisors should not be too ready to fall into this pattern which may well be also of their own choosing. The habit of telling people what to do instead of helping them develop their thinking is still with us. Here, the learner is using the experience of another person as a means of dealing with an unknown task. Learners whose pattern this is, comment on needing more support and certainty initially when a situation feels totally new to them, and say that in the early phase of learning, prescription is what is required. This also relates to past educational experience when a didactic instructive approach was frequently used. Here the supervisor needs to be watchful and judge when this kind of approach is no longer required because the learner has gained greater confidence and adequacy and can rely more on his own ability to explore and understand. The supervisor needs to take special care to ensure that the learner is offered opportunity to expand his own thinking, and does not continue to rely on the 'instruction method'.

Some learners find it useful in supervision to think through in advance and consider the kind of situation and tasks that may confront them. It is an attempt to prepare for a situation before actually being confronted by it. The learner considers beforehand the complexities in a client situation and alternative ways of dealing with these. This is more of an intellectual approach not based on practical experience as the ones already described, though previous work experience is likely to be incorporated. It is termed the 'intellectual preparatory method'.

Some learners function best when using the 'doing first and thinking after' approach. They prefer to go into the new situation with only a minimum of preparation, and to find their way around it, whilst in it. They need to experience at first hand, and can think through the situation only after the event, when they have been involved in it. All clarification is sought subsequently, by means of retrospective thinking. These learners are practical people who need to experience at first hand the feel of the situation. They lack the imagination and experience to do this in advance, but once experienced, can consider alternative ways of helping.

When discussing learning patterns the emphasis must always be, 'by what means does the worker learn best?' What method of teaching is most suited to his pattern of learning? The supervisor should have the skill to assess this and be sufficiently adaptable to gear her way of teaching to the worker's mode of learning, so that learning can be maximized. Whatever the individual pattern, social work learning can occur only when there is opportunity to function and knowledge can be applied by 'doing'. 'Doing', says C. Towle (1954), is a major means to the integration of professional learning. Opportunity to experience change in feeling and attitudes is afforded through planned doing.'

'Get your knowledge quickly and then use it. If you can use it you will retain it,' states Whitehead (1962), while B. Reynolds (1942), comments on the importance of getting the learner quickly into real touch with his material, and to centre his interest on the client. In other words, to start doing.

Motivation, capacity and opportunity

Throughout the discussion so far it will have become apparent that 'the outcome of learning hinges on three sets of factors which are continuously interrelated, the individual's motivation, his capacity, and the opportunity afforded him to attain his aims.' The motivation to go on learning derives from inner and outer needs and is linked with the hope that the activity of learning will bring about the achievement of desired goals. Emotional discomfort does arise at any stage of professional development when the social worker becomes aware that his knowledge and skills are insufficient to meet adequately the demands of practice or the requirements of the job. Dissatisfaction with things as they are produces motivation towards correction and changes.

Along with the social worker's genuine aspiration to understand more about the people to be helped, goes the personal need to master the task, to prove himself and gain greater job satisfaction. 'The more I know what I am about, the more satisfaction I derive from knowing that clients are given good enough help, that I have competence in this sphere and from having this acknowledged by clients and colleagues alike.' The hope of fulfilment compensates for the discomfort experienced in unlearning and learning and adaptations to following in thinking, feeling and doing. The need for physical survival and comfort also enters into motivation. Bread and butter strivings operate for many people in today's society and proof of further learning is frequently required in order to reach higher status and salary.

Yet social workers as a group also have a deep sense of commitment. When this is linked with a learning climate that places value on developing learning, motivation towards becoming a sound social work practitioner is supported and strengthened. Success in learning brings enjoyment in the mastery of new skills and greater competence and increases motivation; prolonged failure in learning leads to dissatisfaction and a decrease in motivation. Past experience is of relevance here, either by engendering hope that at some point the learning will be productive, or by casting doubt upon the efforts ever being successful. The more mature person has a greater capacity for tolerating unmet need, for postponing gratification and for sustaining efforts towards an eventual goal.

The supervisor needs to be aware of these occurrences and facilitate whenever possible the good learning experiences. At certain periods, therefore, the supervisor should clarify with the worker that the acquisition of new knowledge, even the widening of perception will not necessarily lead to immediate useful application of this new knowledge. While it is essential for the supervisor to know this, the worker also has to be aware of this and so avoid unrealistic feelings of failure. The attitude of the supervisor, colleagues and others in the organization is of consequence especially in the beginning of a social work career and can encourage motivation or 'nip it in the bud'.

It has been established that ongoing learning is contingent on the worker's motivation; it is also contingent on his capacity. The term 'integrative capacity' (Dr French, in Towle, 1954) has been defined 'as the capacity of the ego to withstand and master pressure and in particular to channel the pressure of unsatisfied desire into effective goal directed effort.' Towle herself refers to one aspect of integrative capacity as 'this hope engendered power to bear anxiety and tension so that goals may be obtained or abandoned when unrealistic, without excessive cost or damage to the personality.' This ability has its roots in the confidence of the learner established through experience and achievements in the past.

Here integrative capacity is also used to indicate the learner's potential to acquire knowledge, incorporate it and make it part of himself. This is important in social work where proof of development in learning lies ultimately in its use. Since social work supervisors are concerned with furthering the process of integrative learning more detailed consideration will be given to the worker's capacity, a separate yet interlinked element.

CAPACITY

Capacity can be thought of as having four main components; intellectual capacity, physical capacity, ego capacity and the capacity of the social situation. Intellectual capacity relates to the ability to think critically and with purpose; it includes the ability to focus on and think constructively about individual cases, that is, to particularize. At a later stage the ability to generalize is crucial since this enables the transfer of what has been learned from one case to another and so to make wider use of available knowledge. Without this ability the necessary knowledge and skill cannot be systematically increased and social work competence will remain at a low ebb. The capacity to select what are significant and what are trivial factors, to discriminate between the different aspects of the case and accord relevant importance to these is of major importance in diagnostic as well as in ongoing work with clients.

Physical capacity relates to the physical state which affects overall functioning. The reader will know from experience that the general state of health affects the functioning of the total personality. A well person brings confidence and buoyancy to the task. Illness and debility on the other hand are accompanied by fatigue and anxiety. This is discouraging for the learner and militates against integration. Physical capacity includes the total available energy. Robustness is a necessary ingredient for today's social work task, quite as essential as the often stressed sensitivity component. By robustness is meant the physical and mental stamina that is required to deal effectively with client stress and organizational strain in terms of personal repercussions.

PERSONAL DEVELOPMENT AND EGO CAPACITY

Learning in social work affects the whole being; hence demands are made not only on the intellectual or physical capacity but on the emotional state of the individual. Ego strength, in the widest sense, relates to the way the worker comes to grips with reality and the extent to which the personality is able to negotiate the different needs and demands, and selects what is useful between the old and the new. It relates to the personality who is free enough to search for more knowledge and understanding and who is not afraid of losing his identity in this process. It relates to the individual's capacity to cope. G. Caplan (1961) suggests three areas especially relevant in assessing the state of the ego; reaction to stress, problem-solving and adjustment to reality. Reaction to stress is tested by answering questions like how does the person deal with stress, frustration, anxiety? How flexible is he, how resilient? What kind of inner control has he? Is he so vulnerable to outside pressure that he has to shut off in a way that makes him rigid and inflexible, or has he the kind of control that enables him to maintain his balance without having to clamp down too much even when coping with manifold pressures?

Problem solving is the second area for considering the state of the ego. How does the worker solve his problems? How does he cope when there is a threat from outside? Can he solve problems in a realistic way or does he attempt to do this by the use of fantasy, one way of avoiding reality? In extreme cases partial or complete personality disintegration can occur, when the person cuts himself off from the troublesome reality and reverts to a non-thinking state. (The personality is then overwhelmed and gives up; this occurs in psychotic illness.)

Adjustment to reality is a further area for assessing ego strength. Has the person achieved reasonable balance between gratification of personal needs or impulses and reality demands? What kind of compromise has been achieved between personal needs and social demands? What ability is there for the postponement of gratification? How does he handle difficulties? How extensive is his repertoire for coping.

The coping repertoire becomes widened and more resourceful when a person has successfully dealt with a crisis by finding new ways of overcoming difficulties. The capacity can also become extended by education, by being taught how to deal with certain problem situations especially when this is linked with a certain quality of relationship which enables the learner to make use of another's experience because of the trust that exists. This occurs frequently in supervision when the supervisor's experience is available to the worker, when, for example, a supervisory session is used as preparation for working with unfamiliar clients.

The fourth capacity component is that of the social situation needed to support the learner's intellectual, physical and ego capacity in learning. The effort of learning in social work requires support from those in the organization but also from significant people in the more intimate social situation. Emotional upsets at home, worry regarding a wife's illness, or financial worries, add strain to the task and can affect, if only temporarily, the worker's capacity. It is important for supervisors to consider these different aspects that make for integration in learning and to gauge the manageability of the integrative task. The diagram below attempts to illustrate this in another way.

TASK AND CAPACITY

Capacity includes the four aspects that have been considered.

1   If capacity exceeds task by a moderate margin, the learning is smooth. The task becomes interesting and stimulating if demands are made on the

worker's capacity so that he has to make some effort to meet them. If there is a large margin, learning is minimal because there is not enough stimulation.

$$\frac{\quad C \quad}{\quad} \quad \frac{\quad T \quad}{\quad}$$

2   If the task and capacity are about equal, then learning is constricted because energy is being used to maintain the equilibrium, and there is not sufficient left over for creative thinking.

$$\frac{\quad C \quad}{\quad} \quad \frac{\quad T \quad}{\quad}$$

3   When the task exceeds the capacity, then the ego has to protect itself in order to prevent disintegration of the personality, and learning breaks down. The protective function of the ego is operating at the expense of the integrative function; the learner is 'holding on'.

$$\frac{\quad C \quad}{\quad} \quad \frac{\quad T \quad}{\quad}$$

4   The total task may exceed capacity permanently, and this would mean that the worker is incapable of fulfilling the task.

Opportunity for ongoing learning is crucial. The beginning social worker's motivation and capacity are especially dependent on available opportunities to increase knowledge and skill. Supervision provides an important learning opportunity and social work supervisors need to do much vigorous thinking to find better means to support and maximize learning.

Next to the provision of the climate for learning already discussed, the planning, selecting and ordering of appropriate work is most important both in terms of kind and quantity. In order to plan realistically, the current functioning of the worker has to be assessed together with the manageability of tasks (see Chapter 7). To start from the person's own level is relevant to casework and to educational principles. Hence the bulk of a new worker's caseload should consist of selected cases based on the worker's experience and understanding of particular clients. The aim should always be to start with what is familiar and only then to move towards the unfamiliar; to start with what is comparatively simple and then to move on to the more complex. The introduction to new areas of work requires appropriate timing related to a worker's pace of learning. If this is not taken note of the opportunity for learning is missed. The achievement of this is not easy but is possible even in the social services. Adherence to it is easier when the social work team consists of social workers who are at different levels of professional development and who are aware of their different contributions. When all the team members are newly qualified, as is unfortunately often the case, then social work objectives have to be limited so that these are appropriate to what the worker is capable of doing. This clarification of realistic objectives is helpful to the worker as well as to the client, who in any case cannot have his needs met if it is beyond the social worker's capacity, whatever is stated in a case record. This does not mean that there are not times when the supervisor can hurry the pace of the worker or ask challenging questions to encourage further constructive thought and reflection. This important learning opportunity, at present all too rare, is asked for by a great number of social workers who are wishing for a more critical examination of their work, for greater stimulation and challenge. Workers become discouraged and apathetic when they meet with a supervisor's 'fine, you have done it, let's tick it off!'

The integrity of the supervisor is important not only in being a linker and a facilitator in relation to learning, but also by offering the new worker an experience of a professional relationship with the possibility of exploring new avenues and discovering many truths. A good supervisor's model is of the greatest use to the new worker in his work with clients.

6 The practicality of caseload and workload management

Rationing

Human needs are potentially infinite; social services resources are limited and inadequate. Under those circumstances, when demand exceeds supply, there has to be some system of rationing. Such a system should be rational, conscious and declared, rather than be allowed to emerge by default. When that happens 'those who are most easily deterred, least articulate, worst acquainted with the service, least able to wait, or who fall outside the conventional categories of eligibility, will tend to be penalised' (Parker, 1967). Therefore, there is urgent need for the social services department to establish and to declare priorities. Another reason for declaring priorities is to enable the community to have more realistic expectations of this service and what it can provide; for as Parker says:

> the existence of 'universal provision' has unfortunately seduced many into believing that the problem of rationing no longer arises. As a result its political and administrative implications tend to have been sidestepped, and the problem all too often allowed to resolve itself without conscious planning or public debate — often to the detriment of the weakest and the most needy.

Another important reason for establishing priorities is to give guidance to social workers as to how human needs might be weighted, the one against the other. It is important to recognize, as Parker suggested:

> ... that if staff are placed in a situation where they face the prospect of an impossible or unacceptable workload they will find ways of reducing the pressure. They may narrow their conception of the job and its objectives with the consequent danger of red tape; they may adopt uncooperative or deterrent attitudes; they may slow down; suppress information which creates work; go sick or resign. If the organization has no general rationing policy individual workers will have to develop a system of their own, which may or may not accord with the spirit of the service, and may be more or less idiosyncratic.

Meantime, in the absence of a clearly defined priority system, the staff supervisor has to pay particular regard to the hidden priorities of individual social workers. She needs to be aware that there are irrational elements that can enter into a social worker's decision to begin work with a client, to continue to work with a client, to discontinue work with a client.

A worker may tend to elect to work with those clients who respond, make him feel of use, needed and good, even sometimes to the exclusion of more needy clients. It is clearly satisfying to work with clients who engage the worker's interests and sympathy. There is also a tendency for those (workers and supervisors) who have worked previously in a specific field, for example child care, to allow their former interest and competence to become deciding factors in electing to work with certain categories of clients. This is probably unavoidable but needs recognition; it may indeed be a sound basis on which to make decisions relating to work competence, allowing the worker with the highest skill to help a particular client. It is more advantageous for clients and workers to acknowledge the difficulty in taking an objective overall view of client need and to balance the department's service with this in mind, than to deny its existence and force it underground. It is probable that if the social worker's interest and skill were to be given explicit recognition the number of irrational choices would be reduced.

Priorities may also be established because people outside the agency exert pressure to resolve particular problems. For example, councillors may see it as their duty to take an active line of enquiry into some matters: 'They prod and bother' said one social worker. The example of a councillor who urged that the children of a particular family in his locality be taken into care because he found their behaviour unacceptable, is not uncommon and like any other case requires thorough assessment. Even when the social services department is required by statute to offer help to certain categories of clients at certain prescribed periods of time, the assessment of the case, the formulation of social work aims and how these are implemented, will even then depend on the skill and interest of the social worker. The reader may well wish to consider her own reasons, both rational and irrational, for her particular way of selecting.

The supervisor needs to remind herself that when social workers are allocated too large a volume of work, they will define problems as less than they are. She also needs to remain alert to idiosyncratic selection and enable the worker to keep this within reasonable bounds; this she can do by helping the worker acquire the kind of self awareness that moderates personal needs and prevents unnecessary sense of failure or disillusionment. Such reactions occur when social work objectives are formulated without taking into account the knowledge and skill of the worker, availability of time or of material resources.

Caseload management can only be satisfactory when it is part of ongoing supervision, is carried on over a substantial period of time, and when both supervisor and social worker apply their diagnostic skills to the categorizing of clients. The latter is essential to this task. Caseload management is therefore not a mechanical way of proceeding; on the contrary, much thinking has to take place when preparing a diagnostic statement, deciding the aims of treatment and how these can be met, taking into account the quality and frequency of contact. If the original plan based on sound diagnostic judgment cannot be implemented due to lack in resources and the objectives have therefore to be limited, this requires, by social worker and supervisor, explicit comment so that it can be dealt with in future planning. If this were to be carried out consistently, the team and the department as a whole could have an overview of existing resources and those lacking, a useful guide for the planning of future resources. It is useless and misleading to state that a worker is aiming at changing a client's behaviour, when in fact the client is visited once every two months. There also needs to be a periodical review of what has been achieved and to what extent the stated objectives are still relevant or need adjusting. A client who has been seen on a regular once-a-week basis for the purpose of changing behaviour, and whose behaviour has subsequently undergone modification, will still require social work help, possibly of a less intense nature and with reduced contact. When this occurs recategorization of the client in relation to current aims is required.

The application of vigorous caseload management might mean that in some instances a case would not be opened because it can be seen in advance that the objectives cannot be met. Equally, some cases would be closed when the need for help has really passed but the worker may wish to hang on either because 'he likes to keep an eye on things' or because he knows that when he reduces his caseload he may be given others that may well be more formidable, take up more of his energy and time than the one he is holding on to. The advantage of caseload management is that these aspects can be discussed and acknowledged. In order to give ongoing consideration to every case, supervisor and worker are required to keep to a regular review of cases. The diagnosis and the plan should be discussed in the light of the worker's capacity to carry it through. The advantage for the supervisor is a better understanding of the team's capacity and resources. This understanding can be put to use when it comes to case allocation, and when the team members' different contributions need to be taken into account for the benefit of a good client service as well as worker satisfaction.

The supervisor's task in relation to caseload management
Caseload management is best done in the context of staff supervision consistently over a period of time like three to six months. During this practice, supervisor and worker should consider the following points:

1 reasons for opening cases, continuing cases, and closing cases
2 priorities and rational choice
3 the social work aim for a particular client
4 the planned frequency of contact in relation to the objectives; later, see whether this is being maintained, and if not, why not
5 the plan for the individual client in relation to the total workload and whether this is a feasible plan
6 where relevant, other available resources in the community or other people's capacity to help the client, for example, the relevant function of youth workers, health visitors, district nurses, volunteers.

A method of caseload/workload management *Dorothy Lloyd-Owen*
Most social workers have now moved on from talking about caseloads purely in terms of numbers and have been seeking tools with which to manage the amount of work to be done on any given caseload.

In outlining one caseload management scheme that has been applied in social services, probation and voluntary agencies, it is worthwhile to consider why a referral does or does not become a case and also to consider the reasons for closure. The following assessments are suggested as a guide:

Reasons for opening and continuing cases

1 Client has a problem which can be solved.
2 Client has an intractable problem and is causing distress to others who can be helped (others being members of the family).
3 Client has an intractable problem but he will deteriorate if something is not done. He requires support.
4 The client is going to have a problem and needs help in preparing.
(e.g. a foreseeable bereavement)

Reasons for closing cases

1 Client's problem has been solved.
2 Distress to others has been relieved.
3 Support is coming from other sources.
4 The client is sufficiently prepared.

5	The client's problem seems intractable but presents a challenge to the worker.	5	Problem is solved or social worker gives up.
6	Vulnerable clients, e.g. those who have to be on a register like the disabled.	6	Usually none.
7	Social control. (primary task).	7	The period of licence has expired.

The following caseload management scheme requires the social worker and supervisor to categorize each case in terms of objectives based on diagnosis and the social work help required. The objectives can be achieved only when the appropriate resource is available like social work skill, material resource and adequate time. For example: a deprived teenager needing 'mothering' would need to have frequent contact with her social worker if she is to be 'mothered'. A once-a-week contact for instance would make insufficient impact upon her needs. The categories relate to the present social work objectives. As work with the client progresses or the situation changes, cases may need to be recategorized.

The word contact can mean office interview, home visit, in some circumstances, a letter or telephone call.

OBJECTIVE BASED UPON DIAGNOSIS	CATEGORY	FREQUENCY OF CLIENT CONTACT TO ACHIEVE OBJECTIVE
Change client's behaviour. The aim is to bring about change in the feeling area and so to affect a person's behaviour. This requires the opportunity of regular frequent contacts with *one* worker over a substantial period of time.	A	Weekly
Supportive work. Support means to strengthen the client in the situation so that he can continue to function and the situation does not break down. It is concerned with reinforcing whatever coping capacity there is.	B	Two weekly

Helping client come to a decision about a specific course of action.	C	Several times a week, short term.
Caring for the emotionally deprived. 'Caring' here means the offer of a steady nurturing relationship to the immature and emotionally deprived client who has lost out on being cared for in his early life. It is an attempt to repair initial deprivation. It is useless to work with such a client on an irregular basis or when the social worker cannot provide the 'mothering' or 'fathering' so urgently needed.	D	Very frequent often on demand and without appointment, long term.
Changing material environment e.g. change of accommodation or school.	E	As required.
Long term supportive. 'Holding work' prior to starting or finishing work. (see example).	F	4–8 weekly.
Social Control.	G	Weekly.

Examples of the categories:

A Working with a family where the mother colludes in the child's non-attendance at school and where both experience difficulties in separating.

B Working with a blind person, fresh from rehabilitation, and with his family whilst he integrates his new found skills.

C Helping a father decide whether to pursue the question of access to his children.

D Working with clients who have not had adequate parenting, who are chronically unable to manage and who frequently turn up at the office (without an appointment) with yet another problem with which they need help — 'families with problems'.

E Helping a newly arrived family to establish community links.

F   Establishing links with clients in institutions prior to working regularly with them upon discharge. Working with any client e.g. in hospital or in prison towards 'weaning off' prior to closing the case.

G   Supervision of a parolee.

Having categorized a caseload, it is easy to see that a caseload that has a large proportion of As and Ds demands more in terms of skill from the social worker than one that has more Fs, and this is important when it comes to further allocation of cases. Again it is worth saying that as work progresses, and as some objectives have been met the clients will move to another category since the aims have changed.

The next step is to examine whether the caseload can be managed in the context of the social worker's workload, which will also include meetings, supervision sessions, recording, court duties, report writing, travelling time and other duties according to agency function and practice. To examine this it is worth making a plan of eight working weeks, (see Plan pages 86 to 89) bearing in mind that the longest gap between client contacts is in category F — eight weeks. At the top of the plan, write in the names of all clients to be seen in any given week, for example, the As will be included weekly, the Bs, two weekly and so on. The next step is to fill in all the time taken up with meetings, duty days etc, and in the remaining time to work out when all of the clients can be seen; this is usually a salutary exercise!

It is frequently found that the amount of work to be done, based upon the diagnosed objectives, cannot be achieved within the time available; it is crucial then to re-define the objectives rather than assume that these can be achieved with less frequent client contact. Where objectives cannot be re-defined, this scheme can be used as evidence for increased staffing needs.

An additional step, using the 'eight-week plan', is to look each week at the previous week and to note whether the objectives were achieved and if not, ponder as to why not. This exercise frequently reveals a great deal about the agency, as well as the worker; for example, that there were so many new referrals or 'crises' that the regular ongoing caseload was neglected.

Readings from the 'eight-week plan' can show that certain categories of clients are not contacted according to the declared objectives, which should lead worker and supervisor to ask whether the case has been wrongly categorized or whether the worker has in some way avoided appropriate contact due to lack of knowledge or skill or some emotional block; similar questions require to be asked when too much contacting of clients takes place. The actual quality of work will be assessed by means of regular case discussions.

To summarize, this scheme can demonstrate the skill and time needs required in any given caseload. It can show further whether the necessary work can be carried out within the time available in any given week, and is an aid to supervision. Also, it can be used as evidence for staffing needs. Beyond this it throws light on the priority the agency gives to client contact as against meetings or other non-directly client-orientated activities.

This plan relates to the planned work of a probation officer employed in a geographically small, densely populated, London Borough. The officers in the team work on a patch system so that travelling time from one home visit to another is minimal (see pages 86 to 89).

Each probation officer has a regular interviewing night, so that a number of clients are seen by appointment, while others wishing to see the probation officer will know the night when he will be at the office.

A high proportion of the probation officer's time is taken up with preparing reports to Courts (Juvenile, Magistrates, Crown, Matrimonial and Divorce Courts). In the Higher and Divorce Courts there is usually no fixed date of hearing the case and probation officers have to be prepared to attend at short notice for examination by Counsel or others.

On office interviewing nights, appointments are usually spaced at half-hourly intervals. Contacts are regular and frequent. The date of the next appointment is always given, as is also the custom with home visits. Failure to keep an appointment is invariably followed up either by letter or by a visit. Office accommodation enables much more work to be done in the office and home visits are based upon diagnosed need. (Each probation officer has his own room.) Hours of work are long, but annual leave is adequate (six weeks is customary).

The probation service regards case recording as important, both as a working tool and as a legal document in the event of action having to be taken in respect of a client who is failing to keep to the condition of the contract (Court Order or Licence). Records also have to be produced to Home Office Inspectors at times of Area Inspections; hence the specific time allowance each week for recording.

The plan shows the workload of a relatively new probation officer whose caseload consists of thirty-five people needing attention; seven of these are diagnosed as needing contact more regularly than once every two weeks. Nevertheless, in each of the eight weeks between fourteen and seventeen clients have to be contacted if the diagnosed objectives are to be achieved.

The light typeface shows the activity planned, and the darker typeface shows what actually took place with asterisks indicating appointments kept, crosses indicating failed appointments. 'Unplanned' work is also indicated in the darker typeface. SIR stands for Social Inquiry Report. It is perhaps

85

Eight-week Plan showing the workload of a relatively new Probation Officer
Caseload 35   A x 4   B x 18   C x 1   D x 3   E x 1   F x 8

	1 Wk. 3.6.76	2 Wk. 10.6.76
	A BUTT, FIT, STEVE, LEAF. B WALL, HOME, JANE, RISE, O'SHEA, NAVE, WELLS. D CASE, SEW, DINE. E LYE, STANE.	A BUTT, FIT, STEVE, LEAF. B KIRK, DREW, ALLEN, DRAW, MOSES, STRAW. C DIGGER. D SEW. E WHEEL. F LYE, JASE.
M O N	9.30 Admin. relating to workload, letters, phone calls, etc.* 10.30–12.30 Hostel staff group meeting^x **10.30 Called to Crown Court for questioning on Social Inquiry Report.** 2.30–4.30 Supervision Session with Senior. 4.30–7.00 Interviews for Social Inquiry Reports*	9.30–10.30 Admin. relating to workload* 10.30–12.30 Hostel staff group meeting* **12.00–1.00 Office interview – crisis re Fit.** 4.30–7.00 Interviews for Social Inquiry Reports* 7.00–8.00 Moses, Straw visit at hostel.*
T U E S	9.30 Admin. relating to workload* 10.30–1.00 Case recording* 2.30–8.00 Office interviews by appointment. Lye* Wall* Home* Jane* Rise^x Fit* Steve* Nave^x Wells^x Nurse* Mouse* **Leaf*** Kirk*.	9.30 Admin. relating to workload^x 10.30– 1.00 Case recording^x **Saw two new clients and made home visit to Fit's family.** 2.30–8.00 Office interviews by appointment. Sew* Draw^x Wheel* Drew* Digger^x Butt* **Rise*** Nave, Wells.
W E D	9.30–10.30 Juvenile Court duty* 10.30 Evaluation of Probation Officer by Assistant Chief Probation Officer* – 3.00 3.30–5.00 Case recording* **letters to Rise*** Nave, Wells.*	9.30 Juvenile Court duty* 2.30–5.00 Case recording **plus letters to Drew and Digger.***
T H U R S	Duty Officer* – 9.30 2.30–4.00 Meeting of SPO and POs* 4.00–5.30 Home visits, Case* O'Shea* Leaf^x **no reply,** Sew* – 8.00	9.30 Admin. relating to workload* 10.30–12.30 Thinking through and writing Social Inquiry Reports* 2.30–5.00 Case recording* 5.30–9.30 Home and youth centre visits. Allen* **New Client*** Kirk* Steve* Youth Centre* **(10 p.m.)**
F R I	Telephone calls re Butt, Dine.* Write to Stone, all serving custodial sentences.* **Wrote SIR.** 2.30–5.00 Reading time^x letters, admin.* 6.00–8.00 Project meeting*	Telephone call re Butt. Write to Lye and Jase serving custodial sentences* Prison visit including travelling time.* 4.30–7.00 SIR interviews.

3 Wk. 17.6.76

A BUTT, FIT, STEVE, LEAF.
B O'SHEA, NAVE, HOLLAND, NURSE, MOUSE, HOWE.
D CASE, SEW, DINE.
F LEAD, TRAIN, DANE.

4 Wk. 24.6.76

A BUTT, STEVE, LEAF.
B KIRK, RISE, WALTZ, WELLS, HOME, JANE, ALLEN.
C DIGGER.
D SEW, DINE.
E WHEEL.
F HADES, DANE, CART.

MON

9.30 Admin. relating to workload.*
10.30—12.30 Hostel staff group meeting. Cancelled.
Spent morning on phone and recording case notes.

2.00—5.00 Wrote SIR.
5.00—7.00 Interviews for Social Inquiry Reports.

9.30 Admin. relating to workload*
10.30—12.30 Hostel staff group meeting^X Morning spent discussing client with medical personnel.

2.30—4.30 Supervision session with SPO*
4.30—7.00 Interviews for Social Inquiry Reports^X Refereed football match

TUES

9.30 Admin. relating to workload.
10.30—1.00 Thinking through and writing Social Inquiry Reports*
12.00—1.00 Discussion with social worker re FIT.

2.30—8.00 Office interviews by appointment.
Nurse^X Mouse^X Butt^X O'Shea^X Steve* Leaf* Holland^X Sew* Howe^X
2.30—4.00 Case Committee meeting with Magistrates.

9.30 Admin. relating to workload*
10.30—1.00 Case recording^X
Hostel group meeting.

2.30—8.00 Office interviews by appointment.
Kirk* Waltz* Steve* Wheel* Sew^X Wells* Lane^X O'Shea*

WED

9.30 Juvenile Court duty*

2.30—5.00 Case recording*
7.30—9.30 Meeting with volunteers.

9.30 Admin.*
10.00—12.30 School visits to Head and form teachers of clients^X
Juvenile Court duty — colleague off sick.

2.30—5.00 Case recording*
6.00 Meeting re project.

THURS

Duty Officer* — 9.30

12.30—4.00 Home visits, Mouse, Nurse,* Howe.*

4.30—8.00 Home visits, Fitt* Nave* Case* Kirk*
Sew and 2 new clients — finish 9.30.

9.30 Magistrates Court duty*

2.00—4.00 Writing SIRs.
5.30—9.30 Home and youth centre visits. Leaf* Digger* Home^X
Visit youth centre*

FRI

All day visit to a borstal re Train, Dine,* Dane.*

Telephone calls re Butt and Dine. Write to Cart, Dane, Jane, all serving sentences. Letters to clients who failed to appear.

2.30—5.00 Thinking through and writing Social Inquiry Reports^X H/Vs.

87

	5 Wk. 1.7.76	6 Wk. 8.7.76
	A BUTT, FIT, STEVE, LEAF. B WALL, DREW, O'SHEA, NAVE, DRAW, STRAW, MOSES, NORSE. D CASE, SEW, DINE. E LYE, STANE.	A BUTT, FIT, STEVE, LEAF. B KIRK, ALLEN, HOLLAND, HOWE. C DIGGER. D SEW. E WHEEL. F LYE, JASE, TRAIN.
MON	9.30 Admin. relating to workload* 10.30—12.30 Hostel staff group meeting[x] In court re Nurse. 2.00 Visit to HQ. 4.30—7.00 Interviews for Social Inquiry Reports[x] 4.00—6.00 Home visits Digger, Home. 7.00—8.00 Moses, Straw visit at hostel*	9.30 Admin. relating to workload* 10.30—12.30 Hostel staff group meeting* 2.00—4.30 Case recording plus SIR writing. 4.30—7.00 Interviews for Social Inquiry Reports*
TUES	9.30 Admin. relating to workload* 10.30—1.00 Case recording* 2.30—8.00 Office interviews by appointment. Butt* Nurse[x] Mouse* Wall* Lye* Fit[x] Steve* Leaf* Nave[x] Sew* Allen* New clients*	9.30 Admin. relating to workload* 10.30—1.00 Thinking through and writing Social Inquiry Reports[x] Admin., statistics, expenses, letters. 2.30—8.00 Office interviews by appointment. Kirk* Leaf* Wheel* Allen* Digger* Howe* plus 3 new clients.
WED	9.30—10.30 Admin. re workload.* Letters to clients who failed appts. 11.30 H/V Dine* 2.30—5.00 Thinking through and rewriting Social Inquiry Reports* Visited hostel.	9.30—10.00 Reading time. 10.00—1.00 Writing SIRs. 2.30—5.00 Case recording*
THURS	Duty Officer* Office interviews, Fit, Nurse. 2.30—4.00 Meeting of SPOs and POs. 4.00—8.00 Home visits, Drew* Case* O'Shea* Draw* plus brief introductory visits to homes of new clients.	9.30 Magistrates Court duty* 4.00—7.30 Home visits, Holland, Steve,* Sew* 7.30 Visit youth centre*
FRI	Telephone call re Butt. Write to Case, Stane — all serving custodial sentences[x] Visit to prison for preparation of SIR. 2.30—5.00 Case recording and reading time[x] Visits re SIRs.	Telephone calls re Butt and Fit. Write to Jase and Train — all serving custodial sentences[x] Off sick. 2.30—4.00 Visits to Head and form teachers re Holland, Waltz, Rise[x] Off sick.

	7 Wk. 15.7.76	8 Wk. 22.7.76
	A BUTT, FIT, STEVE, LEAF. B HOME, JANE, O'SHEA, NAVE, WELLS, NURSE, MOUSE. D CASE, SEW. F LEAD, CART.	A BUTT, FIT, STEVE, LEAF. B KIRK, DREW, WALTZ, DRAW, ALLEN, MOSES, STRAW. C DIGGER. D SEW, DINE. E WHEEL. F DANE.
M O N	9.30 Admin. relating to workload* 10.30—1.00 Case recording^x Letters to those in custody and school visits. 2.30—4.30 Supervision session with SPO* 4.30—7.00 Interviews for Social Inquiry Reports* 7.00—8.00 Visit Moses and Straw at hostel*	9.30 Admin. relating to workload* 10.30—1.00 Case recording.* Office interview Fit* 2.00 Visited accredited volunteer re client. 4.30—7.00 Interviews for Social Inquiry Reports*
T U E S	9.30 Admin. relating to workload* 10.30—1.00 Thinking through and writing Social Inquiry Reports* 2.30—8.00 Office interviews by appointment. Fit^x O'Shea* Steve* Nave^x Sew* Home* Wells^x Nurse* Mouse*	9.30 Admin. relating to workload* 10.30—1.00 Thinking through and writing Social Inquiry Reports* 11.15—12.00 Magistrates Court with client. 2.30—8.00 Office interviews by appointment. Butt* Drew* Steve* Leaf* Sew* Draw^x Digger^x Moses* Straw^x
W E D	9.30—4.00 Visiting client in prison including travelling time* 2.30—5.00 Case recording.* 5.00—6.30 Office interviews with new clients.	9.30 Allow nearly whole day for visit to client in prison including travel* Reading time*
T H U R S	Duty Officer.* Wells* Nave* 2.30—4.00 Reading time^x 2.00—4.30 NAPO meeting. 4.30 Home visit, Leaf* H/V Fit.	9.30 Magistrates Court duty* 4.00—8.30 Home visits. Lane, Kirk, Waltz, Wheel, plus new clients*
F R I	Telephone call re Butt and mother of Lead. Write to James Lead — all serving custodial sentences* 2.00—3.00 Meeting SPOs and POs. All afternoon borstal visit Cart^x 3.00—5.00 Writing SIRs.	Telephone calls re Butt, Dine, Dane, all of whom are serving custodial sentences* Case recording. 2.30—5.00 Case recording* plus writing SIRs.

89

more helpful to prepare the plan for work to be done and then, on tracing paper laid over it, indicate what actually took place.

As will be seen from week one, most of what was planned was achieved, except for a weekly hostel staff group meeting which had to give way to the priority demand to attend Crown Court; three people failed to keep their appointments on the Tuesday (and were given further appointments the next day), whilst two came without appointments; one planned home visit proved abortive. In all quite a satisfactory week if the content of the interviews was consistent with the objectives.

Week 1 can be contrasted with week four, where five specific pieces of work were not carried out as planned. Again the hostel staff group meeting was not attended (one must ask what priority does this officer give to this meeting since he did not attend on five out of eight planned occasions), although later on the Monday, and again on the Tuesday the hostel was visited in preference to interviews for Social Inquiry Reports and case recording. On the Wednesday, Court Duty had to take precedence over planned work. However, the writing of a Social Inquiry Report was fitted into Thursday to enable home visits to be made on the Friday to clients who had failed to keep their appointments the previous Tuesday and Thursday.

On balance, this probation officer has a manageable workload with sufficient time space in which to re-arrange the workload, and to fit in unplanned visits to make up for planned ones that did not take place.

Introducing caseload management into the agency *Joan Hodgets*

SETTING

My placement as a 'student senior social worker' was in an area social work unit which, pending the organization of the social services department, was concerned with providing a service for the mentally ill, mentally handicapped, physically disabled, elderly and the blind. The two workers I supervised had mixed caseloads and each had a responsibility for providing a service for a large number of people on the register of blind persons. When I began supervising they both expressed some resentment at the amount of time they felt they had to spend on blind people because of the statutory obligations and what they felt to be unrealistic expectations of the local voluntary association for the blind. They commented that they were continually being called upon to do things which were not appropriate for social workers and although admitting that they did not in fact visit many of the people on the register they felt nevertheless under a great deal of pressure because of these large numbers for which they were being asked to provide what was felt to be a questionable service. It was therefore agreed we should apply a caseload management scheme to their problem.

My own feeling at this time was of some doubt as to the usefulness of this exercise, but since both workers had expressed a firm wish for help in managing their caseloads, I felt I should look at this with them.

WORKERS

Worker 1 was a widow of middle-age who had formerly trained as a medical social worker but had never practised in this field, working as a Probation Officer for a short time after training and before marriage. She had returned to social work after her family had grown up and become independent of her. For a time she had worked for a voluntary association concerned with the elderly and then joined the social work unit.

Worker 2 was a young married woman with a sociology degree who, prior to joining the social work unit, had worked as a mental health social worker in another authority.

STAGE 1

My first step was to ask the workers to classify each of the cases on their active work load — I suggested that in the first instance it would be better to look at this section of their load and to set aside the 80–100 cases they each had who were on the register of blind persons but whom they had not in fact seen. I allayed some of their anxiety regarding these clients by putting it to them that it was highly likely that if they were in any real need of help they or someone else would get in touch with the unit.

I explained to both workers that I was attempting something of an experiment with them and decided to ask them to put their clients into one of the following categories:

A Changing behaviour	Weekly contact	e.g. Helping a newly handicapped person adjust to his disability.
B Supportive work	Two- to Four-weekly contact	e.g Helping a mentally ill person to remain in the community.
C Helping to reach a decision	Frequent contact — short term	e.g. Helping an unmarried mother decide whether or not to place her child for adoption.

91

| D | 'Caring for' emotionally deprived | Frequent contact — long term | e.g. Playing a parent substitute role to a family with multiple problems. |
| E | Changing environment | Contact as required | e.g. Helping an old person towards admission to an Old People's Home. |

However, as they both felt there were cases on their load which did not fit into any of these categories, I agreed to these additional six categories:

F	Long term supportive	e.g. supporting elderly — who by and large are managing four to eight weekly intervals.
G	Annual statutory visits	e.g. to people on register of blind persons.
H	Service visiting	e.g. taking craft material etc., to blind clients.
I	Crisis visiting	e.g. to people whose mental illness flared up.
J	New cases	
K	People seen but not yet properly assessed	

The classifications made by the social workers were:

	A	B	C	D	E	F	G	H	I	J	K	TOTAL
Worker 1	1	10	—	2	5	12	—	—	—	—	1	31
Worker 2	3	5	1	2	2	15	3	6	1	3	1	42

STAGE 2

I then looked with the workers at the time available for visiting — counting each half day as one session.

Worker 1 was employed for *four* days per week only. She spent half a day each week on intake duty and half of an afternoon each week was taken up by staff meetings. She had fortnightly supervision sessions which took about half of a morning and the same amount of time was spent at a club for the blind which she attended. This left her with six sessions each week in which to do visiting, recording, correspondence, telephone calls and various administrative duties.

Worker 2 was employed for *five* days per week. She spent an afternoon each week on in-service training seminars, a day each week on in-take duty, about half a morning each week at supervision and the same time at weekly staff meetings. She was also, therefore, left with six sessions for visiting etc.

STAGE 3

As neither social worker had formed the habit of sending appointments to clients and seemed to find the idea of looking ahead to make an estimate of visits over the month too threatening, an exercise I had originally hoped they would carry out, I asked them instead to enter on a chart the minimum visits they felt they were able to make during the following week. They then returned this to me at their next supervision session with relevant alterations showing what had in fact been their week's achievement.

STAGE 4

When the charts of achievement were returned to me, I marked off the visits they had made in a register and noted when the next visit was due according to the worker's categorization. I then took up relevant observations gained from this at our next supervision session.

At the end of an eight-week period I gave the workers a chart of their rate of visiting and we discussed some of the implications.

SOME OBSERVATIONS

At Stage 1 the workers seemed to be helped to get their caseloads into perspective. This also gave them an opportunity to make some form of diagnosis and helped me, as their supervisor, to get some knowledge of their cases. The mere fact of going through the load resulted in the closure of a few cases not seen for many months.

At Stage 2 the social workers were helped to see what time they really had available for visiting. They both expressed some surprise at how much of their week was taken up by duties other than seeing their own clients. See Chart 1, p. 94.

At Stage 3 an attempt was made to help the workers plan at least a week ahead. By asking them to commit themselves to state the minimum they expected to achieve they were helped to feel some form of achievement especially when they exceeded this number of visits. Both workers said they were reluctant to make written appointments with clients because so often they were diverted to various crises and would feel guilty if a client was expecting them and they were unable to get there. Some of this feeling about constant diversion proved to be a reality.

Chart 1 — worker's weekly plan

	A.M.	P.M.	Evening
Monday	In / Take	In / Take	
Tuesday		In-service Training	
Wednesday		Staff Meeting	
Thursday	Supervision		
Friday			

At Stage 4 it became evident that there were some cases where there was no match between the rate of visiting and the worker's categorization (see Chart 2, p. 95). With both workers this was most apparent with the A cases. Worker 1 visited her case only once during the eight-week period and Worker 2 did not visit one of her A cases at all during this period. When this observation was taken up with the workers each gave an explanation about their pressures and geographical problems but, even when a definite attempt was made to organize a week's visiting round these cases, they found some reason for not going. It then became very evident that there was some block; this then had to be taken up.

With Worker 1 the problem was that of bereavement. The worker said she had intended to help the client over the period of mourning, but in fact by the time she had made her visit the woman had begun to make some normal adjustments.

With Worker 2 the problem was that of a mentally handicapped child. The worker recognized that the mother of the child needed a great deal of

Chart 2 Number of visits made to clients during 8-week period 11th January – 5th March 1971

WORKER 1

Categories from caseload	A	B	C	D	E	F	G	H	I	J	K	Total clients seen	Other Visits	Grand Total
	1	10	–	2	5	12	–	–	–	–	–			
January														
12–15	–	4	–	–	3	3	–	–	–	–	–	10	6	16
18–22	–	–	–	–	–	2	–	–	–	–	–	2	1	3
25–29	1	3	–	–	–	2	–	–	–	–	–	6	4	10
February														
1–5	–	3	–	–	3	1	–	–	–	–	–	7	2	9
8–11	–	–	–	–	1	1	–	–	–	–	–	2	4	6
16–19	–	4	–	1	1	–	–	–	–	–	–	6	3	9
23–26	–	4	–	–	–	2	–	–	–	–	–	6	1	7
March														
2–5	–	3	–	–	–	2	–	–	–	–	–	5	2	7
TOTAL	1	21	–	1	8	13	–	–	–	–	–	44	23	67

WORKER 2

Categories from caseload	A	B	C	D	E	F	G	H	I	J	K	Total clients seen	Other visits	Grand total
	3	5	1	2	2	15	3	6	1	3	1			
January														
11–15	1	–	–	2	–	2	1	–	–	–	–	6	4	10
18–22	1	1	–	2	–	1	–	1	–	–	–	6	4	10
25–29	1	1	–	2	–	–	–	–	–	–	–	4	–	4
February														
1–5	1	2	–	1	–	2	–	1	–	–	–	7	4	11
8–12	–	2	–	2	–	–	–	–	–	–	–	4	1	5
15–19	–	3	–	1	–	–	–	–	–	–	–	4	2	6
22–26	–	1	–	1	–	1	–	–	–	–	–	3	6	9
March														
1–5	1	2	–	1	–	1	–	–	–	–	–	5	6	11
TOTALS	5	12	–	12	–	7	1	2	–	–	–	39	27	66

Other visits These were to clients not on caseload at beginning of 8-week period — many never went on active caseload.

help. She commented on her fear that if she visited once again the woman would begin to unburden herself, would be needing intensive help that the worker did not feel she had either time or skill to give.

As a result of our discussion the mother was referred to a group for mothers of handicapped children from which she subsequently benefited.

The D client of Worker 1 had a change in situation, being admitted to hospital, and thus did not need the visiting by the worker.

One of the D clients of Worker 2 improved with intensive visiting and was eventually recategorized.

When looking at the F cases it became apparent after discussion with the social worker that many of these could be closed once a visit of assessment had been made and the client had been left with the knowledge that he could approach the department if further assistance was needed. It also became apparent from looking at this area of their load that many of these clients would be better served by an alternative service such as a club or regular visiting by a voluntary worker. This information was given to the divisional social worker who used it as evidence when requesting extra provision of resources.

Both workers were surprised to note how little service visiting they did in fact do and were able to say that it was not the number of visits as the type of service they were asked to provide, which they resented.

At the time of categorizing, Worker 2 had three new cases to whom she had made initial visits for the registration of blind persons but whom she had not visited again during the eight weeks to follow. There were other cases which needed to be discussed and so we agreed that during the next weeks we would look at one of these cases each session as well as consider one of the F cases which she felt needed discussion prior to being closed. She was eventually able to say that she was reluctant to close a case as this usually meant she was then given a new referral which would take up far more time.

At the end of the eight weeks the workers were very ready to classify the new cases on their load, to reclassify others and to continue to supply me with the relevant facts of their visits. The pace of taking up the various problems which became apparent was slow; other anxieties unrelated to this particular exercise came up and needed attention and this task had to be left till the next time.

I continued with the same method throughout my stay in the agency. Again, various problems concerning workers' skills and defence mechanisms became apparent, as did some of the department's organizational weaknesses and lack of necessary resources. One example, was the need for a service other than that of a social worker to take craft materials to the blind. The social workers did not always count these deliveries as visits on their returns; they did not wish to give a false impression, as often the time spent was minimal, though travelling time could be considerable.

CONCLUSION

On returning to my own agency and attempting to adopt the model of caseload management described above to a generic service, I have discovered a number of different facets and each time the model has been used by other interested senior colleagues they have brought to it their own interpretations, adaptations and modifications. It seems that once the basic concept of measuring caseloads by quality rather than quantity is agreed and accepted, the pieces of the model can be moved about and, rather like a kaleidoscope, different patterns can be identified upon the angle from which you decide to view.

For example, if you are a team leader or a senior responsible for the servicing of a geographical area, you can use the information gained by the categorizing of your team's caseloads as evidence of staffing needs, e.g. if there is an overall high percentage of A and D cases this would indicate the need for skilled caseworkers, whereas if the overall pattern is one of caseloads top heavy with F cases this would imply that what is required is additional assistance from good calibre staff, not necessarily qualified, who can relieve the caseworker of a number of long term supportive cases; in some instances at least, give a more meaningful service to the client because they recognize their role as supportive rather than therapeutic.

By examining closely with a worker, or group of workers, any one particular category of case it may become apparent that the amount of time spent by the worker(s) with clients with certain kinds of problems is disproportionate to the client's need for casework and is really a propping up due to lack of material resources. The gathering of evidence of this type can then be used by the team to indicate to the policy makers that material assistance is what is really required. An example of this is the unsupported mother whose real need may be for an opportunity to have her child cared for by an effective day care service so that she can supplement the family income as well as gain stimulus from the company of adults. Another example relates to the families on low income who suffer a drop in income during school holidays because their children do not then receive a free mid-day meal. It would be more economical for these families to receive some form of assistance, in the form of provision of groceries than for a social worker to have to double her rate of visiting to help a mother with her anxiety over how to make ends meet.

Although any form of caseload management inevitably takes up time which might be used for other things the majority of workers and supervisors who have taken part in caseload management have found it a useful exercise. They have derived from it a sense of being in control over their caseloads and in varying degrees have been able to develop some management techniques in respect of balanced and tolerable workloads.

In order that any caseload management model is meaningful, the social workers concerned must be truly involved and must come to see that far from being an instrument to turn social workers into battery hens it is a tool that can help them keep from unnecessary pressure and allow at least for some free range thinking and activity concerning the way they tackle the very complex and diverse problems they are facing, particularly in the social services.

A look at three workloads *Susan Smith*

The principles of caseload management, of balancing clients' needs with existing resources, has been discussed. I propose to take the discussion further into workload management and to give consideration to the total demands made on the social worker's time. Apart from the caseload, what other demands are made on social workers? What other tasks make up the workload? And how does a worker or a team decide priorities?

Working as a senior with multiple responsibilities for a team, for liaison work and with a complicated caseload, these were some of the questions and problems that presented themselves during the first year following amalgamation and finally resulted in taking a close look at these three workloads.

The social workers' inability to cope seemed to be a matter of great urgency. Anxiety and depression were uppermost; social workers were feeling under tremendous pressure but were also concerned that they were no longer offering as good a service to clients as they used to 'In the good old days.' In order to get through their work, they found that they had to work long hours. I found myself wondering whether this was a true situation and if so, how it had come about. Was this pressure realistic? Where did it come from, what was new, and how did it relate to client demand or administrative demand? Could the pressure be created by anxiety and frustration brought about by the introduction of the generic approach which meant working in unfamiliar areas not of the worker's choosing? While cases tended to get left, the anxiety in the social worker increased; the periods between visits became longer and eventually it was possible for the case to get 'lost', though the anxiety remained with the social worker. If cases are such that they cannot be left, must have priority, but the motivitation of the social worker is low, this produces conflict and frustration in the worker who feels that she is neglecting her 'true clients'. Motivation is an important factor in how the social worker manages both caseload and workload.

In order to look at pressure caused by increased client demand, a record of all new referrals was kept over a six-month period as well as of the referring agency. It was found that letter referral did not increase dramatically; in the area of mentally handicapped children referrals even decreased. However, the number of self referrals, callers at the office, increased considerably. This was a realistic cause for social workers' anxiety who were still unfamiliar with some of the presenting problems. Often social workers were unable to say 'no' to clients although they were fairly sure no help could be offered. At the same time there was also awareness of the team's problems in accepting more ongoing work resulting from a duty call. One difficult problem presented on a duty day, could upset the planned work for the following two days.

The pressure created by increased administrative demands was also considered, and it was found that provided records and statistics were kept up to date these had not increased significantly. It seemed that the anxiety was within the social worker who had to learn new procedures or whose records were not up to date.

Having considered these areas of demand, it was decided to look at the actual planned workload that was undertaken by some social workers. How did they use their time? Two examples are illustrated below: one, the only man in the team at that time, and another, about whom there was some concern.

The method used was time taken for tasks over a period of four weeks. Some meetings lasted about four hours but were only held once in four weeks; therefore 1 hour in each week was allocated for such a meeting. It was agreed that on average each interview took about an hour and therefore four clients seen weekly took up four hours of social work time. For clients seen once in two weeks the time was also averaged to a weekly commitment. This it was felt was the most satisfactory way one could attempt to measure the social worker's time commitment without this becoming too complicated.

EXAMPLE 1 – This social worker was the only man in the team at that time and therefore tended to have on his caseload young adolescent boys in care or under court supervision orders. He also dealt with any referral when it was felt that a male worker was required. He was a newly trained worker, normally with lots of energy and enthusiasm, with real caring for people and with particular interest in young people. Now he complained of not coping, of being disillusioned and misled by his course. Below is tabulated his workload for the average week. There was a constant problem of recording. His supervision sessions he used well.

Regular office commitments	*Hours*
Day duty	8
Staff referral meeting	$2^1/_2$
Divisional meeting and inservice training	$2^1/_2$
Supervision	$1^1/_2$
Court attendance and escort duty	$2^1/_2$
Intermediate treatment meeting (monthly)	1
Psychiatric consultation (attendance irregular)	$^1/_2$
	$18^1/_2$

Mixed caseload of 47
24 adolescents who have been before the Court

(a) 4 newly home on trial	seen weekly	4
(b) 6 home on trial	seen fortnightly	3
(c) 9 in County residential establishment	seen 3-weekly	3
(d) 5 in residential establishment outside the County	seen 3-weekly	2
		12

He attempted to see the parents of
(a) fortnightly	2
(b) monthly	$1^1/_2$
(c) 3-monthly	3
(d) 6-weekly	1
	$7^1/_2$

Of the 24 adolescents he identified severe marital problems as a contributing factor to the boys' difficulty and attempted to see 6 couples at least fortnightly

2

Also included on his caseload were the following clients:
Elderly confused	3
Elderly	10
Mentally ill	4
Mentally handicapped	3
Physically handicapped	3

The community anxiety was high regarding the elderly confused and apart from telephone contact with others concerned he saw clients for about 45 minutes per week. $1\frac{1}{2}$

His only other regular commitment was to a mentally ill man seen fortnightly $\frac{1}{2}$

    2

This makes for an average total working week of forty-two hours.   42

Travelling time, recording time, office and telephone duty, rota duty at night and social inquiry reports for courts were not included in the forty-two hours.

Much of his work of necessity had to be done in the evenings. This workload management study threw up many problems. In the first place it reassured the worker that his feelings of pressure were realistic and that it was unreasonable to expect him to cope with such a workload. This worker had envisaged regular fairly frequent contact with his adolescents. What had not been foreseen was the amount of casework to be done with the parents and families. By right these should have been counted as two separate client groups on his workload.

Travelling time was a big factor, especially when visiting boys in special establishments outside the county. This had not previously been recognized. The worker felt that these boys needed regular contact, yet the time taken up in travelling meant that this was one of the first areas to be sacrificed, causing distress to the boys and concern to the worker. Of necessity a number of this worker's appointments were in the evening, either with parents or boys who were working during the day. The degree of evening work that was being done could have meant that the pressure went unrecognized. However, once acknowledged, much of the current pressure still had to be coped with as the hours of work could not at that time be substantially decreased, but it became quite clear that no further work could be allocated to this worker.

EXAMPLE II was the workload of a social worker about whom the whole team showed concern. This worker had complained for some time, of inability to cope, of there being too much pressure on her from all kinds of sources; she also appeared depressed. Her anxiety and depression were demonstrated in the amount of time she spent talking about her feelings to colleagues who were much affected by her mood.

Regular office commitments	Hours
Duty day	8
Staff referral meeting	2½
Divisional meeting and inservice training	2½
Supervision	1½
Group supervision	1½
Marital interaction (inservice training)	¾
Community resources group (monthly)	1
Psychiatric consultation meeting	1½
	19¼

Mixed caseload of 57	
Mentally ill (one group of 5 and one hostel group of 3)	8
Mentally handicapped	4
Blind	11
Elderly	14
Physically handicapped	2
Children in care	2
Fostering	3
Miscellaneous	4

Regular commitments	Hours
2 groups of 1½ hours each	3
plus preparation time	1
1 elderly blind seen weekly	1
2 care orders seen 3-weekly	1
3 mentally ill seen 2-weekly	1½
	7½
This makes for an average total working week of	26¾

From an examination of this workload it can be seen that the work pressure experienced was unrealistic in terms of the actual work done; in fact she was hard pushed to put in a full week's work. From discussion with her group supervisor it appeared that a similar picture was emerging: the worker was coming to supervision groups ill prepared or did not appear at all. Recording her cases had been one area of alleged pressure, and although a number of half days at home with a recording machine had been allowed, this really was time wasted as it produced almost nothing. The worker was unable to record even then.

The value of this workload study was the evidence produced that the pressure experienced by this worker was not due to the quantity of work undertaken. It provided an opportunity to examine where the pressure came from and opened up other areas for discussion. It led to the worker's recognition that she herself required help and that for the time being she was not in a position to help her clients. The recognition of this was a tremendous relief for the worker as it was to her colleagues.

Discussion on these two workloads raises questions regarding responsibility for overseeing and for being more aware of how social workers are working. Obviously the allocation of supervision time here was inadequate for help with caseload and workload management and for regular discussions on social work method.

It was the senior's responsibility to vet referrals, allocate work and attempt to keep the balance fairly even within the team. It was also to a large extent the senior's responsibility to meet the community, e.g. general practitioner, health visitors, and to liaise with hospital teams and voluntary committees. There was a need here to balance the community's demands with what the team could supply.

Most seniors will be familiar with the feelings of being caught between headquarter's expectations and policy and what the team can cope with in reality. Seniors too will be familiar with the pressures they themselves feel when the team does not function adequately, perhaps because one or more members are not working to full capacity. These were the points that came up for consideration, that had not till then received adequate attention, and it was therefore considered useful to look also at the senior's workload (see page 104).

Perhaps all three workloads show to some extent the changing role of the social worker. In 1969, when the National Institute for Social Work Training examined social workers' caseloads in the health and welfare departments, it was noted that on average only one hour's overtime was worked per week. In those days caseloads in this locality averaged between 60–65; yet although the numbers have since been reduced to 40–45, social workers were working longer hours.

Apart from the demands of office duty previously unknown in health and welfare departments, social workers' roles have widened. Increasingly social workers are expected to be able to offer alternative choices of help to clients in the form of casework, group work and community work. To attempt to meet these expectations social workers are searching continuously for further training. In addition, the organizing and supporting of volunteers requires extra knowledge and skill as well as time; so does liaising with hospitals, residential establishments, magistrates, and the police. This raises serious questions for the supervisor in terms of

Senior social worker's caseload

Overall total 48 hours

MONDAY	TUESDAY	WEDNESDAY	THURSDAY	FRIDAY
1½hrs supervision	1½hrs supervision	½hr occupational therapist consultation	½hr supervision	1½hrs supervision
2hrs student supervision	1¼hrs assess mtg.	1hr old people's home	¾hr supervision	1½hrs supervision
2hrs old people's home	2hrs staff mtg.	1hr divisional staff meeting	1½hrs psychiatric consultation	2½hrs divisional meeting for senior staff
2hrs mental health hostel	2hrs geriatric hospital	½hr consultation with psychiatrist in subnormality hospital	1½hrs county meeting	1½hrs handicapped client
2¾hrs evening group mental health hostel	½hr manic depressive client	1½hrs handicapped client	1½hrs 2 elderly in own home	½hr mentally-ill client
2hrs seeing clients at old people's home		½hr mentally-ill client	1½hrs handicapped client	
			½hr mentally-ill client	
12¼ hours	7¼ hours	5 hours	7¾ hours	7½ hours
½hr travelling time	2hrs travelling time	2½hrs travelling time	1¼hrs travelling time	2hrs travelling time
12¾ hours	9¼ hours	7½ hours	9 hours	9½ hours

Not included

Dictation or general administrative work
Dealing with 51 other cases
Dealing with proper vetting of new referrals
Looking at overall caseloads
More time should have been spent at mental health hostel and at the unstaffed mental health hostel
Rota duty

104

dilution of work and her responsibility to workers. At what point does the supervisor have to say, not even one more case can be taken on by this worker even at the expense of a client, otherwise none of his work is going to be of quality and use to any of his clients?

It becomes clear that more evidence has to be produced for purposeful thinking so that it will be possible to declare what can be done but also what cannot be done by a social worker or a team.

GENERAL CONCLUSION

Social workers in social services departments face the difficult task of controlling demand. The range of client service for which the social services department is now responsible is so wide and numbers are too large for every client to get the required help from overloaded social workers. It is therefore essential for social workers and supervisors to be clear what can be done in each particular case and to clarify objectives. It is also necessary to discuss these at an early stage with the client and to make quite clear to him what help can be given, its nature and quality. This requires clarity as to what is possible, organizational skill, by which is meant the ability to calculate in advance the time required for different commitments, diagnostic skill for rational decision-making, honesty and courage to declare essential client needs that remain unmet.

Caseloads demonstrate the use of time as between different clients; workloads demonstrate the use of time as between client service and other organizational requirements. It is especially important for the supervisor to consider if this balance is reasonable, and if necessary, to make adjustments. When too much time is spent in meetings, social workers are prevented from getting on with the primary task.

The reader is encouraged to compare the number of cases on the probation officer's caseload with the caseload of other social workers and make his own deductions. The probation officer's interviews are regular, of short duration and take place mainly in the office, a very different pattern from most social workers in social services departments.

The supervisor needs to ensure that her own workload is manageable and that there is sufficient time available for her primary tasks of supervision, allocation of work and liaising, especially with policy makers.

The supervisors workload here demonstrates that the role is too broad, and the functions too diverse; this prevents her from doing her job effectively. While it is essential for supervisors to carry a small caseload, this must not become the supervisor's main and primary function. This is one of the distinctions between social workers and social work supervisors.

7 First assessment of the level of social work functioning*

The establishing of an assessment of the present level of social work functioning of a social worker is as important as the building up of a client's psycho-social diagnosis. Though the aim and the focus are different, there are many similarities concerning methodology.

The purpose of an assessment of social work functioning is to understand how a worker operates at the present time in his work situation; to know his educational state in relation to his social work task; to know what quality of help he can extend to what range of clients; to identify what he does well, what he does badly. It is extremely important to have a picture of the social worker's performance and functioning. In the first place, how the worker functions on the job affects crucially the kind of service he is able to extend to any one client. It is of no use to client, worker and agency, if on paper the client's needs are said to be met when in reality these can only be met to a limited extent because of the low level of functioning. The supervisor's perception of a worker's functioning should affect the kind of case allocation. Attempts must be made to match client needs with worker's skill.

The first reason for an assessment of the level of present social work functioning is to establish in what way and to what extent the worker can help certain kinds of clients at this particular point in time. A further reason is in relation to the the worker's own learning needs. Only when these are known can appropriate learning be provided. The supervisor is one of the main opportunities.

To understand the supervisor's specific function in relation to a particular worker, an assessment of the worker's professional development has to be made. What are his areas of knowledge? What knowledge is lacking? What knowledge can he apply in social work practice? What knowledge can he not yet apply? What skills have still to be acquired or further developed? This *should* determine *what* a supervisor teaches.

An understanding of a social worker's learning pattern should determine *how* this is best taught. People's learning patterns differ; some will want to

*often referred to as 'educational diagnosis'.

go into the situation and learn while in it, others may feel more comfortable to prepare themselves in advance for what they may find when visiting a client. Knowledge of the stages of learning linked with an understanding of the social worker's work experience acts as a guide in knowing *when* to teach *what* and how long it may take before this knowledge can be applied in practice.

In a sense, the distinction I have made between client needs and worker needs in relation to the establishing of an assessment of the level of social work functioning is somewhat artificial in the sense that the one feeds into the other. By making an assessment the supervisor appraises the present capacity of a worker. When such an assessment has been made in relation to every worker in her team, she will know the resources within her team. Good supervisory practice not only meets the professional needs of the social workers in her team but enables the expanding of team and agency resources.

Thus, the function of a first assessment is to clarify the functioning of individual social workers, primarily in understanding and helping clients.

Since a worker does not operate in isolation but is affected by the culture of the department it is important to take stock of these features and their effect on individual social workers. It is necessary, therefore, to take a look at the organization and the special way in which it operates. It is necessary for the supervisor to be clear about what are established practices and procedures, about the freedom of operation but also the constraints; to be aware of the all-pervasive climate, supportive in one instance but not in another; the availability of certain learning opportunities but not of others.

One cannot look at the worker in isolation but has to consider his work practices in relation to that of his organization; as on a football ground one has to see the performance of all the players and the condition of the pitch in order to comment on the particular skill of one footballer. A supervisor must understand when a worker's way of operating has more to do with idiosyncratic behaviour and when it stems from agency practice; for example, when the automatic acceptance of a referral from a general practitioner by a social worker represents departmental practice and social workers are not expected to make their own judgement as to the appropriateness of a referral, or when it relates to the individual response of a social worker.

Recording is another example. When a worker is assessed in that area of work, the state of his recording will to an extent reflect the practice of the whole department.

Equally when assessing a worker's ability in relation to helping a client with a housing problem, the general mood of the agency, the depression that is often experienced by all in relation to this type of request, must be taken into account. This generalized feeling of helplessness, arising from a situation of inadequate resources, affects also the worker who has not yet had personal experience of working with clients in this predicament.

When a worker declares to the new supervisor that all his cases are going smoothly, that he does not require discussion, one has to wonder if this signifies his resistance to declare what he is or is not doing, but one also has to ask questions about the climate of the agency and to what extent the shelving of supervisory sessions is generally condoned. The worker's performance has to be viewed within the context of the organization, its culture and practices.

The assessment of a worker's present functioning must take note of the social worker's past personal and work experiences, since these will influence current functioning. Experiences from the past are usually carried around like personal luggage and it is important to identify the different articles and their uses in the present work setting. Sometimes these articles may hinder rather than help. The example of a worker, who on becoming a member of the social services team demonstrated how he undervalued himself in relation to colleagues and showed his uncertainty when approaching clients, revealed, during sympathetic exploration with his supervisor, that this pattern had first emerged in his family, when he had always undervalued himself in relation to his siblings, and had felt of little account. This pattern again emerged in his performance as a social worker, when his low estimation of himself in relation to others was affecting the manner in which he did respond to clients.

It is useful to gain understanding in what circumstances these pieces of luggage were acquired, how long they have been carted around, and under what conditions there might be less need for them. The above example demonstrates that some acquired attitudes can be dysfunctional both to the work and to the worker.

The illustration given in detail in Chapter 5 demonstrates the opposite. This relates to the example of an experienced worker in a new agency who found himself face to face with a resistant client who was mourning the loss of her own worker and demonstrated her reluctance to talk to the new one. This social worker found that he could transfer the knowledge and understanding gained in his previous setting about clients' feelings at losing a trusted worker, and by his sensitive handling enabled the client to begin to think of him as a possible helper. This worker's sensitivity, a combination of empathic understanding and good previous agency practice, was the kind of luggage which would be useful in all kinds of different work situations.

The formulation of a first assessment has to take into account those features that are:

1 largely idiosyncratic and belong to the worker — this includes the worker's past experiences as these affect present attitudes, behaviour and performance
2 those features that relate mainly to the stages of learning and not to individual learning blocks. Certain areas of complex knowledge can be assimilated only gradually; hence there exists a lag between knowledge learned and when this can be consolidated, integrated and transformed into useable skills
3 those features that belong to the culture of the organization.

How then do we proceed in a practical way on making a start and building up a first assessment? Like anything worth doing, this building up is a lengthy process requiring careful analysis of *all* the social work tasks undertaken by the worker. The picture must include what the worker can do, what the worker cannot do; what tasks he can carry out with competence and in what areas he is lacking. The first assessment must indicate his relative strength and weakness. The supervisor needs to produce the evidence in the form of data consisting of observation and comments that can be demonstrated by looking at the interview. Observations relating to the interaction between worker and client can be clarified in the supervisory session when a reflective dialogue takes place. Any assessment must be supported by evidence. Hunches by themselves are not good enough. A thorough assessment is a time consuming process. The initial picture is bound to be incomplete and it is only gradually, over a period of weeks, that a picture can be built up of how a social worker operates in his different work areas in his organization.

Obtaining the evidence is the first step (see models); the next step concerns the meaning of the evidence. For example, a social worker appears consistently unable to assist people in a crisis situation, we note this down (first step) and then (as the second step), ask what the reasons for this might be. Is it lack of knowledge and understanding about people in crisis situations? If it is lack of knowledge, then knowledge is what the worker requires for better practice. However, his inability to help could be related not to lack of knowledge but to blocks in the area of feeling; thus the questions to be asked are, does the worker not feel for people in crisis? Does the worker feel too much for people in these situations? Is he perhaps attempting to protect himself by refusing to see the total situation? In that case, the learning block is related to feelings and the focus in supervision must be directed on to these areas. Lack of resources, can be another reason for help being ineffective and for the worker feeling discouraged from the start. By resources are meant not only material provisions but the kind of supportive structure that a worker requires if he is to meet fully and in a helpful way the stress and strains of some clients.

The steps are quite clear. Data has to be collected and assembled. This data can be clearly demonstrated, and can be called evidence. Then, questions are asked about the meaning of the evidence. The understanding of the meaning of the evidence makes clear the focus and the task of the supervisor, that is, how the supervisor can help the worker to become more competent in his weaker areas of work. The objective of the first assessment is to clarify the level of the worker's professional readiness to function. Areas of weak functioning are noted but competent work areas are also highlighted, often to the surprise of the worker. The advantage of a first assessment shared between worker and supervisor is that both know where they stand, what can be achieved at the moment and what the goals are for the future. The worker does not have to pretend that he is competent in areas when in fact he feels unable to cope with certain categories of cases or complex situations. Different models are offered for the collecting and assembling of relevant data. These are the kind of data required in order to make meaningful statements about social workers functioning in relation to social work skills. Global statements without specific evidence are not good enough. Having done this, the supervisor can begin to build up a picture of the worker's performance; she is likely to find that the worker functions well in some areas but less well in others. She will then have to consider what the reasons are for poor functioning, whether it is due to lack of knowledge, lack of experience, lack of feeling, or over-involvement in feeling: the answer to these questions will spell out the supervisor's task, whether the availability of knowledge is more important than the recognition of difficulties in the feeling areas. What is essential is the understanding of those factors that hinder competent work performance.

When the picture has thus been filled in in a detailed way, the supervisor is then in a position to consider areas in a more global way, for example, social work skills. (See also, areas for assessment in Chapter 8 'Evaluation'.). The supervisor can then make a statement backed by evidence about the worker's ability to:

1   understand clients and assess material and emotional needs
2   formulate a realistic treatment plan
3   evaluate relationships with clients and to recognize and acknowledge those he has difficulty to work with.

This is only a start; so far only the area of social work skill in relation to direct contact with clients has been considered.

The same process will have to be undergone in relation to other important work areas. For example, the knowledge of social provision will be an area for consideration, the manner of recording will have to be looked at, the whole area of workload management, i.e. the worker's ability to assess priorities in planning work, his ability to handle emergencies and operate under pressure while also allocating time for non-urgent work, must be clarified and assessed. All these areas are of prime consideration in the total functioning of a social worker.

The importance of establishing a first assessment cannot be overstressed. The reluctance of supervisors to assess workers stems at least in part from the fact that it is difficult to know how to proceed and how to develop a system that can be seen as being fair and objective. The way towards objectivity is to collect evidence that can be seen by other people, and certainly by the worker. This evidence can then be jointly examined and commented on; if feelings and hunches are the only things that operate in a worker's assessment, then the supervisor's reluctance to get on with this important task can be readily understood.

To encourage and enable the supervisor to start on the task of building up a first assessment, four practical models are presented here. It is suggested that these be viewed as guides to be used creatively to undertake this new and important task. Most supervisors will wish to find their own style in evolving this tool for sound supervisory practice.

The first model, Assessment A (see pages 112 and 113), relates to the building up of evidence of a qualified social worker after an initial period of only five weeks. It is suggested that the reader start by reading and considering the column headed 'The worker — areas of work' — then moves towards the next right hand column — 'The Worker — past personal and work experiences' — then considers the content listed under 'Agency' and 'External Factors'.

The last column to be considered is the one on the extreme left, headed 'Supervisor's exploratory questions'. These questions relate to the total written data. This is an important column and demonstrates the supervisor's thinking.

Model A: First assessment of the level of social work functioning.

A new supervisor begins to build up the evidence for a first assessment after five weeks of supervision. This data relates to the area of work with clients. After *qualification* the worker returned to the department where he

Supervisor's exploratory questions	THE WORKER *Areas of work with clients*
	Relates well to new clients who declare their need of help e.g. Mr Snooks and Mrs Jenkins
What knowledge has he of the concept of ambivalence? How does their uncertainty make him feel?	Demonstrates impatience with new clients who have mixed feelings about seeking help e.g. Mrs Carter and Mr and Mrs Williams
Likes to feel they agree with him? Needs to feel accepted.	In ongoing work copes best with conforming clients see family X and Y.
What makes him feel so much in relation to these children? Is it knowledge of what they need or does he identify with this situation because of his own experience?	Has shown understanding and caring in relation to Johnie and Charlie both in an institution. Visits regularly and without fail
Does he lack in feeling or does he feel too much? Is he overwhelmed by these problems?	Has a tendency to think of clients in terms of categories and numbers. Remoteness
He has little knowledge of normal phases e.g. lacks knowledge of the normal adolescent questions, doubts and rebellious feelings	Gets very irritated by fairly normal adolescent behaviour. Says he did what he was told at their age, why don't they? Arthur and Norman
Why can he not look at the client in his total situation? Does he not want to see those areas where he is uncertain that he can help? Has knowledge how to obtain practical resources	Finds it difficult to look at the client and his total situation. Tends to look at one aspect only. More ready in offering concrete help than anything else
Why did he drop these cases who were in need of help in sorting out complex relationships? Has he a limited idea of the function of the social services department? Does he lack knowledge and perception of how to deal with relationship problems? Is he afraid of working with feelings?	Has dropped cases A. B. C. after only a few interviews. Did not consider they needed help. All three cases had relationship problems.

had previously functioned as an unqualified social worker. He had now been qualified for eleven months. There had been no regular supervision prior to the new supervisor's arrival.

THE WORKER	AGENCY	EXTERNAL FACTORS
Past personal and work experiences		
Was in the regular army for a number of years. In many ways liked it, 'You knew where you were'. Qualified as a social worker eleven months ago. Had a placement with what sounds an inadequate supervisor. Says he felt at a disadvantage on the course because he did not have an academic background.	Still somewhat chaotic following reorganization. Many people uncertain about their roles and functions. Minimum support from colleagues — many of them preoccupied with what is happening to them. No previous regular supervision. Is allegedly responsible for 95 cases.	Pressure from GP group, who frequently comment on the good old days when they had good contact with a small department. Critical comment from Clerk of the Court about social workers who do not know how to behave in court. Good relationships with the housing department. Cases in need of housing are felt to be a joint responsibility.
Lost his mother at an early age. Brought up by father and maiden aunt who considered it 'her duty' to look after her sister's boy. Visits father only occasionally and only for short periods.		

Model B: First assessment of a social work assistant after 3 months (see p. 117)

Personal	Worker's previous experience and luggage	Agency
Married middle-aged woman, in her mid-50s.	Home Office Welfare Course in 1941.	Very poor accommodation.
Seemingly secure marriage.	Welfare Officer during the War 1946 linked to Services.	Confused contradictory leadership.
Grown-up family, good contact.		Conflict with Head Office.
Husband recently retired and they talk freely of reversed roles — many hobbies, gardening, boating, wine making.	Since then high management and organizational jobs.	Poor relationships within agency, also with outside agencies. Development of such not encouraged.
The youngest by many years in her family, regards nephews and nieces as brother/sister age group — seems to have good contact with them.	Coordination of Voluntary Services.	Unclear role definition, throughout.
	British Red Cross.	Understaffed with a history of rapid turnover of staff.
Pleasant sense of humour.		

Strength, skills and capacities		Weak areas: gaps in skills and knowledge
Extensive knowledge of voluntary organizations. Extensive knowledge of local resources.		Inclined to identify with clients by showing personal bits about herself, for example, how she felt as a child in a similar situation; or giving the example of a friend in a similar position to the client).
Sound common sense and does not panic. Empathy with clients and is not judgemental.		

Ability to recognize how clients might see her (e.g. Mum role, which she did make use of when working with two adolescent sisters on court supervision for non-attendance at school, she could see value in being the positive, approachable 'Mum' a role which the natural mother could not fulfil).

Ability to look at herself. Ability to pursue and persevere.

Likes to set goals for herself and see her role clearly. Can be consistently firm with clients (e.g. Mc C family, W family. In her role with the W family which had multiple problems she consistently saw parents together and in financial budgeting she was a great asset to them).

Has intuitive casework qualities (recognizes the need to build relationships, in order to influence the outcome e.g. W. O'D family. The latter was a complicated private foster situation; while recognizing agency anxieties she formed a very positive relationship with a frightened, threatened private foster mother first which enabled her then to move into other areas for discussion.

Thinks about what she is doing.
Can take anger and temperamental personalities.
Keen interest in what she is doing and desires to learn.
Well organized in her work load generally.
Can recognize attempts to be manipulated but needs help to cope.

Has a tendency to talk across one and may miss the client's contributions, as seen in supervision sessions.

Needs help to recognize where the client is and that the client's pace may differ from hers.

Perhaps at times too definite, forthright, bordering on 'giving advice'.

Needs knowledge of basic principles of work with clients e.g. interviewing, confidentiality.

Recording
Sees value in keeping records.
She is up to date and factually correct
Letter writing is good.

Recording
Needs help in laying out initial interviews and information so that it can be used for quick reference. They tend to be very factual and express only a little of the feelings involved, though discussion is different.

Worker's attitude to supervision	Supervisor	Planned help
Very positive response. Comes well prepared. Always punctual and material provided in advance. Often starts on practical issues but increasingly is testing herself to look more closely at casework. Has accepted my suggestions for reading and acted! Can contain anxieties very well really. No apparent difficulties regarding an age difference.	Need to protect her from conflict higher up. Need to be clear and firm regarding my role and responsibilities. Need to be available. I have difficulty in deciding my expectations — perhaps I expect too much and am inclined to forget she is untrained. Selection of work is difficult. If we had more trained staff how would this worker be used — perhaps this is an area where supervisors need help from peer groups to consult and clarify expectations.	Induction course to see wide range of service-field, residential, financial etc. Case presentation and discussion. Draw out and build on the very strong intuitive element in this person. Social Work Assistant Group to look at theories and principles of casework and the skills and tools necessary for the job.

This attempt at a first assessment gave the basis for sharing with the worker the very positive parts of her skill and knowledge which she brought to the job and the way in which she could use them. She was a middle-aged, married woman with experience of life as wife and mother, she had certain areas of training and special knowledge which were also relevant but I thought she also had intuitive skills. The assessment also helped to highlight those areas which needed special thought and help and these were used fruitfully. She joined a small group for basic social work discussion, she read, and used opportunities available for groupwork discussion. This worker progressed rapidly and after nine months was working with fairly complicated problems most successfully and was upgraded within a year to being an unqualified social worker.

Model B
The second model, B (see pages 114 and 116), relates to the first assessment of the level of social work functioning of a social work assistant.

Like the previous model it also is concerned with the worker's previous experiences for the purpose of understanding this worker's mode of operating and his particular pattern of learning.

In this model, work performance is already divided up into areas of competent and not yet competent functioning. In the area of recording e.g. it is immediately apparent what the worker is doing well (left-hand column). The right-hand column shows up what is missing, and points to the areas where supervisor and worker have to do further work.

A special section is allocated to questions relating to supervision — in particular the worker's attitude to supervision, supervisory tasks including questioning about the supervisor's own difficulties in setting appropriate standards for this worker, and how she herself might get further help with this. She comments also on the difficulty of selecting appropriate cases so that this unqualified worker can give real help to selected clients but at a time when there is a shortage of qualified staff.

Model C
The third model C (see pages 118 to 124) is set out somewhat differently. Relevant facts concerning the worker's background and experience are noted and a number of detailed examples and illustrations are given relating to work performance.

Some supervisors may find this a more manageable model. This supervisor asks herself many questions in relation to the meaning of the evidence of the work performance; she also asks questions about her own supervisory performance and whether she is offering the most appropriate help to this worker. This reflective questioning by the supervisor concerning her attitudes, knowledge and skill is yet another good reason for noting down carefully the many factors that contribute to the building up of a social worker's assessment.

Model C: A first assessment of the level of current social work functioning of one social worker with evidence of how an assessment is arrived at

Relevant factors in assessment:

'Inner' e.g. past experience of worker	*'Outer'* e.g. agency
Initial motivation for an early career in nursing, e.g. doing things for others.	7 years' work in children's department and social services department with almost no supervision.
	Uncertain of role in reorganized department as compared with non-developing children's department.
Growing up and leaving home by own children.	Lack of common ground with colleagues — age, academic background, values, qualifications.
Rigid, materially poor childhood with dominating mother and similar upbringing of own children.	Challenges by colleagues of previously accepted principles within the department.
Super-ego and authorization parts well developed — husband a 'special' constable.	No relevant academic knowledge. Much greater period of working in area so greater knowledge of people, practices, etc.
Age — mid 40s	
Limited educational experience and so of intellectual development.	
Partly due to external factors, strong motivation to respond to supervision but also because it illustrates positive aspects of her capabilities as a social worker.	

Assessment of the level of social work functioning
1. Work with clients
2. Work with others
3. Work management
4. Learning

SUPERVISOR'S REFLECTIVE THINKING	1 WORK WITH CLIENTS
How far insecurity about own security or lack of knowledge and skill? (A question I repeat frequently)	Immediate and warm response regardless of client's situation. Frequent offers of material and practical help without proper assessment, as seen in a number of cases, e.g. the W family, young family with very large debts in spite of husband's *high* and *regular* wage. The social worker is wanting to pay off debts instead of looking for reasons for their existence.
Needs to be liked unduly? Fears rejections?	A further example are the Bs where the teenage boy in this single parent family was enuretic, and social worker provided sheets, blankets, etc. and did not look for causes of enuresis and possible treatment. Inability to cope with clients whose needs not obvious to her — rejects or creates needs, e.g. Mrs S. Perception of real material needs usually good, e.g. the Bs, low income family whose children distressed going to school in shabby and inadequate clothing.
Why do I continually fail to make progress here? Why inability to take a total view? Very strong identification is lacking in other areas of work from which she shies away.	Very poor perception of interaction of family or groups.

Assessment of parents and children is always based on her own nuclear family, e.g. T T a teenage boy who wanted to go to the pop festival. Social worker could only make a |

	decision by looking at her own teenager's previous request to do this and not by looking at TT's situation. A further example is that of C, an adolescent foster child whose foster parents are strict in their demands. Social worker could not work through the attitudes of the girl nor the adults but could only state the hour she had set for her own teenagers to be home without reference to the different home situation. Beginnings of seeing relevance of own behaviour and reactions on clients, e.g. WS and her over-protection of money giving. Willingness to use most other agencies for benefit of clients, except schools.
Needs reinforcement when taking initiative in this area because of occasional rebuffs in the past and lack of own educational experience. Lack of confidence in self and failure to see relationship in itself as a tool.	
A fear of rejection?	Serious failure to involve clients in reaching goals, e.g. Cath E: insufficient preparations regarding foster home. Inability to end relationships with clients, e.g. Mr B — elderly gentleman previously living in appalling conditions. Rehoused in wardened flatlet, supported by home help and volunteers and no longer needing social worker's help, but she could not let go. The WS were a family where repeated efforts made to help but uncooperative and no improvement in situation. Social worker continued -to visit, drink tea and chat in -neighbourly manner and agreed she could not give social work help but

SUPERVISOR'S REFLECTIVE THINKING	
I do not suspect any deep/ unhealthy fear but lack of support in efforts. I must be more conscientious in attacking this.	repeatedly made excuses why she could not close the case that week. Very little exploration of feelings with clients, e.g. breakdown of foster home after 16 years. Social worker helped girl find lodgings but did not look with her or with foster parents at their feelings.
Lack of precision and clarity of purpose of visits.	Not very good fact gathering; tendency to 'chat with old friends'. Often necessitates return for vital information.

SUPERVISOR'S REFLECTIVE THINKING	2 WORK WITH OTHERS
	Social work with colleagues Clerical staff Ancillary staff Residential staff Other agencies Supervisor
Some insecurity of own position.	Over-identification with own agency and tendency to stereotype others.
In part involves her status and fear to let others be more involved with clients in case of rejection. Historical result of office development and her background sharing more with clerical staff. Needs help in seeing her contribution to office team.	Difficulty in examining roles of others, e.g. family aids, volunteers, residential staff. Identification with clerical staff rather than professional colleagues but some progress in becoming part of social work team. Very good relations with clerical staff; in some aspects other social workers could use as model. She had worked with the clerical staff for several years and her attitude to them was that of a colleague, asking appropriately for forms, files, secretarial help. Some other social workers carried out

Very positive use although not always conscious how she is using supervisor, e.g. parent figure. How far should I pursue?

Am I being too gentle in not tackling reports more forcefully?

their tasks demanding these services in a way in which they would not approach other colleagues inside or outside the department. Works as individual social worker rather than in cooperation with team, e.g. liaison with housing department, schools, etc. Relationship with supervisor good, although at times over-dependent. Not always clear about apppropriate use, e.g. will phone on Sunday about minor details but needs help with Court reports which she does not ask for. Does not bring personal problems when inappropriate, but did use supervisor when crisis over husband's employment interfered with work.

SUPERVISOR'S REFLECTIVE THINKING

I find it difficult to approach when these practices were part of formative years in social work. Try to tackle when right time — have started. I fear destroying.

Real concern and warmth for clients — fear of failure and rejection.

Poor management of time and lack of confidence and discipline in committing to paper.

Never previously criticised. Again I must not destroy all of which was considered good in past but I must tackle it at the right moment.

3   WORK MANAGEMENT

Wastes time, e.g. does not make appointments as a rule; does not prepare interviews, so vital information is not always gained; does not work as member of team.

Reliable if arrangements for visiting made.

Records not up to date and often too much irrelevant material.

Reports not written with sufficient thought to purpose — Court report on RA (15) reads in part like woman's magazine story.

In some areas she is beginning to leave Bertha Reynolds' phase 2 and is entering 3. This is noticeable with the Be family. Here the social worker is at times no longer just keeping up with the situation but is starting to understand what is happening, yet not usually able to do anything about it. She perceives the effect that the mother's attitude and family experiences have on the adolescent son but does not appropriately pursue. In other areas supervision has resulted in return to phase 1. Reflection and rethinking make for a high degree of self-consciousness and non-automatic responses.

Indication of capacity of openness to new ideas in some areas but worker still acts without attempting to understand and control. The council house situation for the Be family was one such example. The social worker was active in influencing the housing department in allocating a council house which would affect work with family, but she did not understand the full implications; nor did she control her contact with the housing officer so that she mis-represented the case. This, in the long run, could lead to future difficulties in relation to other cases where the housing officer's help will be required. Increasing recognition of own activity and its effect and on occasions she is able to control this.

Need to take this at her pace. Not a value previously considered.	In relation to the ws, the worker is beginning to realize that she is using money-giving because she feels unable to offer anything else. Although she responds to new ideas and knowledge it takes a long time to integrate and use. Needs repeated discussion. Some denial of relevance of self awareness for practice or at least much slower development in this area.

Model D

Model D (pages 126 to 137) demonstrates the continuous building up of an assessment of the level of social work functioning of an unqualified worker (who was a social sciences graduate) which began in the first month and became more comprehensive during a five-month period.

It is suggested, as with Model A, that the reader starts by considering the column headed 'Worker', 'Previous experience of worker and luggage' and 'Worker's personal events and comments'. Then to move onto the column providing 'Evidence'. Then to consider the content under 'Agency' and the effect of agency climate upon this worker's functioning. Finally, to give consideration to the supervisor's questions and activities, and to what extent the reader is in agreement with the questions asked and the activities that were undertaken.

Model D: building up of a first assessment of the level of current social work functioning of an unqualified social worker

AGENCY	WORKER'S PERSONAL EVENTS AND COMMENTS	PREVIOUS EXPERIENCE OF WORKER AND LUGGAGE

Internal
The various area offices of the new Social Services Department were geographically widely spread; teams were formed in name, but the members of any one team remained in their various original office settings for some time; therefore little team identity, supervisors had to travel about in order to supervise.
Accommodation poor, cramped and badly situated in terms of accessibility to the public.
Real lack of resources at many levels, e.g. telephone, shorthand typists, interviewing rooms and residential accommodation.
The pattern of client contact is by means of home visiting due to very inadequate interviewing facilities.
Repeated new procedures for

Both parents died just prior to her going to university.
She has older siblings, one studying for a profession.
Married. Husband mentioned without communicating any impression of him as a person in relation to self. No children.
She described herself as having 'very early inability to stand up for herself'.
Constant undervaluing of herself.
Inability to accept that she might be valued by her clients.
Needs to feel she is 'in-command' of situations, but when faced with the knowledge that this is not so, tends to opt out, using poor health as an excuse for not coping.

Commenced in mental welfare department as a trainee but left after a short time to undertake a social science degree course at university.
Had a placement in a renowned psychiatric hospital.
Worked in a hospital for subnormals in an administrative capacity.
Inability to discuss feelings and attitudes *or* a lack of emotional experiences.
Implicit emphasis on good manners and respect for parents/authority.
She joined welfare department as welfare officer just prior to Seebohm reorganizations — no supervision was available. Emphasis of the department then was on material giving. Chose then to work with the elderly and physically handicapped.

WORKER	EVIDENCE	SUPERVISOR'S QUESTIONS/ACTIVITIES/ COMMENTS
This worker was 26 years of age. 1 Her main experience to date has been to provide practical help for the elderly and physically handicapped. In this area she is extremely competent. She has good knowledge of social provisions for the elderly, physically handicapped and the mentally subnormal. She speaks with understanding and concern about Old Folks Homes and the difficulties experienced by the matrons. She has some, but less, understanding of the difficulties experienced by the old in giving up their homes. Of late she has been taking the old folk to view prospective homes prior to making decisions, or has tentatively taken matrons to meet hospitalized prospective	She originally chose to work in this field where she considered that her capabilities matched the standard of work then carried out by the welfare department. This is a new practice for her and demonstrates new understanding and growth.	Since she functions well in this area, I can bear it in mind when allocating new cases and concentrate on her work with other client groups and needs. I must also ensure that other workers in the team get some proper experience of working with the old and physically handicapped. This area of work demonstrates her capacity to feel and learn where she feels secure and interested.

AGENCY	WORKER'S PERSONAL EVENTS AND COMMENTS	PREVIOUS EXPERIENCE OF WORKER AND LUGGAGE
recording and statistics emanating from the research section and imposed upon the social workers. Contacts with clients recorded in superficial terms; the inadequate secretarial help contributes to the department's poor standard of recording. The department is trying to improve and has set up a working party to examine this whole subject.		

WORKER	EVIDENCE	SUPERVISOR'S QUESTIONS/ACTIVITIES/ COMMENTS
members prior to admission to their homes.		
2 Evidence of little social work knowledge and skills apart from above. Had no teaching or experience in social work processes.	This shows up in the totality of her approach to working with other than those described above. Doesn't know what a social history is or how it relates to diagnosis — talks about casework but has no knowledge of its meaning. Frequency of contact is not related to client need. Has no experience of working with adolescents; no understanding. One would think she has not gone through adolescence herself. Is distant and judgemental when she describes an adolescent on her caseload, e.g. described 16 year old Betty as hard, sophisticated looking older than her years and promiscuous, on no real evidence. No appreciation of norms, for example, clothing or leisure time interests and activities.	I must explore with her the contents of her university course and placements. Is she the right material to go on a C.Q.S.W. Course?

AGENCY	WORKER'S PERSONAL EVENTS AND COMMENTS	PREVIOUS EXPERIENCE OF WORKER AND LUGGAGE
Recently introduced in-service training, catering for large groups of across-the-board staff; a didactic lecture-style method used in the main with learners playing a passive role. Training so far orientated towards explaining Acts. The department has tried to be 'generic' without the members of the hierarchy having a necessary balance of 'generic' experience between them; this has led to delays in policy and decision making, resulting in insecurity of social workers. General atmosphere of pressure. The department is in a depressed state. Staff use much energy on 'survival' following reorganization; little left over for working with clients. Ex-welfare department social workers have very high caseloads, are perceived by others as being least professional.		

WORKER	EVIDENCE	SUPERVISOR'S QUESTIONS/ACTIVITIES/ COMMENTS
Her focus is almost exclusively on practical help with very little awareness of the emotional content of such intervention.	Miss H a middle-aged high grade subnormal living with disabled relatives, called upon SSD for help with aids. She recognized help could be given to Miss H and in second visit many months later, endeavoured to impose a good plan for her development onto the unprepared, anxious relatives. Failed to pick up their doubts, and could not explore with them alternative solutions.	Need to help her plan with rather than for.
Very good observational ability, yet unable to use it. Some concern expressed in supervision session in relation to future plans for a girl's care, yet, unable to communicate this concern to the girl when it was needed.	e.g. RF teenage client in care and feeling rejected by family and at times by staff of the home. She cares about this girl and her future yet constantly employs judgmental responses to all of her expressed unhappiness and conflict. Records faithfully her non-verbal, distressed behaviour but makes no use of it in the interviews or in future planning, e.g. when the girl, in her presence, tried to overhear a	What is her capacity to feel?

AGENCY	WORKER'S PERSONAL EVENTS AND COMMENTS	PREVIOUS EXPERIENCE OF WORKER AND LUGGAGE
This worker falls into this category.		
Lack of foster homes; poor response from the community despite strenuous efforts made to expand this resource.		
Pressures from doctors on one side and clients on the other because of severe lack of Part III accommodation, e.g. old age people's homes. Never-ending new referrals.		

WORKER	EVIDENCE	SUPERVISOR'S QUESTIONS/ACTIVITIES/ COMMENTS
Feels distinctly unable to cope with the very verbally aggressive mother of teenage client. Again inability to empathise, plus lack of confidence.	matron as she thought speaking about her, her response was 'Didn't anyone ever tell you eavesdroppers hear no good of themselves?'. Has repeatedly voiced this in supervision sessions. The difficulty is exacerbated by her feeling unsure of how she can help the girl, coupled with lack of residential resources. Accepts without questioning the mother's criteria of good and bad caring in terms of physical conditions only.	The fact is she cannot as yet cope with this woman, therefore a second worker will have to be involved.
Her whole deportment is usually tense and unbending. She functions on extremes, showing a desire to 'give' when confident of acceptance.	When unsure of what to do, she withdraws from contact either emotionally during an interview, or by failing to make regular contact, e.g. in a case where the wife has terminal illness and her husband knows this, has arranged practical care and planned to close case upon death of the wife. Also, in case of late middle-aged couple where husband became	Check on frequency of contact is a good indicator of how competent she is feeling in a case — watch out for unnecessary over-contacting. She is having an awful time, especially when she becomes aware of her inadequacy in a case. This creates anxieties in me — can I help her enough, even quickly enough? Her need to 'survive' herself makes her opt

WORKER	EVIDENCE	SUPERVISOR'S QUESTIONS/ACTIVITIES/ COMMENTS
	aphasic, saw the need to arrange for speech therapy only and then cease contact, didn't recognize in either case that partners required help. When sure of what is needed and she can supply it, e.g. with the confused elderly requiring practical help, she will visit daily even.	out of situations she cannot cope with.
3 Values supervision Looked initially for teaching in a passive way. When she felt more valued as a person through having regular time given to her own supervision, began to contribute some ideas of her own. Demonstrates very real lack of personal emotional experiences *or else* is very repressed and defended.	In early supervision session stated 'they mean so much to me, as it is the first time I have had a chance to think about what I am doing'. (See column 3). Later asked to be able to learn more about adolescence.	So much to be done, where shall I begin? I fear hurting her by too direct confrontation of her vast areas of lack of knowledge and skill. My dilemma is when to 'put in' and when to 'draw out'. It is largely the former, but when I felt she had been given some framework I considered she could have been more active. When I tried to help her use her own experiences of being an adolescent, for example, I found that either she had repressed these or somehow had not had any of the usual ones!

WORKER	EVIDENCE	SUPERVISOR'S QUESTIONS/ACTIVITIES/ COMMENTS

4 No idea *re* caseload management. Reluctant to part with cases. Feels she is managing her high caseload. She has no real criteria for opening and closing cases.	Caseload 112, states 1 case requires weekly contact, 7 fortnightly, 10 short term intensive contact, 76 monthly contact, 18 unspecified. The actuality was:
	    5 × weekly
	    4 × fortnightly
	   10 × monthly
	   19 × 2 monthly
	    5 × 3 monthly
	    9 × 4 monthly
	   31 × 6 monthly
	   21 × yearly
	    8 × no contact listed.
	More than 50% seen 6 monthly or less. (See chapter on caseload management).
		In any event caseload is too high for her or anyone. I need to endeavour to reduce caseload to a realistic level. Can any of her cases be dealt with adequately by welfare assistants?
		Is she reluctant to reduce quantity in case this might lead to higher expectations of quality of work?

5 Inability to cope easily with authority figures, tendency to 'give in' even when it might work against the clients' interests. Assumes these feelings are common to colleagues (partly true), but hers are more extreme.	Has allowed herself to be 'bullied' by admin. figure controlling a residential resource into not pressing for her client's proper priority. Tends to act upon instructions of home help organizer, psychiatrists or doctors, by doing visits when they tell her to and 'proving' the point they feel they have made.	No real professional identity as yet. I need to do a great deal more teaching, using new allocations which could be more acceptable.

WORKER	EVIDENCE	SUPERVISOR'S QUESTIONS/ACTIVITIES/COMMENTS
6 Poor judgment relating to lack of knowledge, skills and inability to empathise.	Dealt with the question of a helpless old man accepting residential care in such a way that he declined. Accepted his answer as realistic, made no arrangements for his care over a weekend, with the inevitable results that he had an accident and was admitted to hospital.	She seems to have unintegrated ideas about client self determination, yet I know she cares in her own way about this man. I need to discuss this with my supervisor since we are ultimately accountable for errors of judgment she makes whilst she is learning.
7 Lack of useful records upon which to base supervision sessions. She has no real knowledge or evidence of the value of good recording. However, she has demonstrated capacity to learn in this sphere.	This is related to general low departmental standard of recording. A requested process recording was originally written in the form of a dialogue, with no comment about non-verbal interaction. Process recordings have improved recently through her being willing to be taught.	Teaching her how to process records has been a useful way of getting her to think more broadly about what is happening between her and clients. Written evidence causes me to move backwards from where I thought she was to where she actually is in many respects.

WORKER	EVIDENCE	SUPERVISOR'S QUESTIONS/ACTIVITIES/ COMMENTS
8 Lacks objectivity. Takes clients' feelings 'personally' rather than 'professionally' because of blocks in perceiving clients' implicit emotional stress. Really an inability to empathise.	Accepted intellectually that a deprived teenager might have anxieties about meeting a 3rd social worker, but became hurt, angry and insecure when client initially failed to keep appointments.	This is still all to do with lack of professional knowledge and identity.
9 *Colleagues* Relates reasonably well but not closely to peer group colleagues. Sees herself as *subordinate* to people further up the hierarchical ladder, and is therefore unable to be appropriately critical of failings within the system, despite feeling strongly about some, e.g. inappropriate content of assessment forms relating to admission of an old age person to a home.	Neither on very good or poor terms with peers because of her minimal interaction with them. Came back from an in-service training course on the structure and communication system of the department with the 'knowledge' that she was a 'subordinate' employee! Feels unable to join colleagues in taking issues about stand-by duty although she agrees with their arguments.	The physical setting precludes useful interaction. It is hard for her to feel other than subordinate whilst she has so little to offer as yet, especially in view of departments low estimation of 'ex-welfare officers'

8 Evaluation

The nature of evaluation
The purpose of supervision is to ensure a standard of service to clients and to provide appropriate help in relation to problems. The purpose of evaluation is to take stock of past practice and to look forward to what remains to be done. In a previous chapter, consideration was given to the importance of a worker's first assessment. Evaluation is the periodic assessment of a worker's functioning and capacity and follows on from the first assessment of the level of social work functioning. A first assessment is required in order to be able to evaluate six or nine months later what has been achieved in the period between the first assessment and later evaluation and what still remains to be learned.

Evaluation is a part of supervision. It is an ongoing process and cannot be implemented outside supervision. A kind of evaluation takes place in each supervisory session when there is some stock-taking of particular areas of work. In each supervisory session work performance is discussed and examined. Frequently areas of competence are recognized and sometimes areas are pinpointed where not much movement has occurred. New connections are noted and hindsight is being developed. By hindsight is meant the worker's own ability to reflect on what he might have done but has not yet been able to do in practice. The concept of hindsight is commented upon in the stages of learning and relates especially to stage three when practice skills can be seen to lag behind intellectual understanding.

Since in each supervision session work performance is considered, when it comes to an evaluation session where the worker's total performance is looked at, nothing completely new should come up. There should be no unexpected revelations. The primary task of evaluation is to review all aspects of the work and to gain an overall view of quality and quantity of the total workload. In this sense it is quite different from a supervision session when time can be appropriately used to discuss one or two cases only.

'Evaluation implies a judgement based on a standard' wrote Virginia

Robinson (1936). In the subsequent discussion however she comments on some of the factors that make the establishing of a standard a very complex task.

The complexity arises because of the difficulty of measuring and comparing some social work skills. Those related to concrete social work tasks can be measured and compared with relative ease. Other social work skills, the more subtle ones, are less easily comparable. It is much easier for example to assess and compare workers planning of time and the implementation of the plan than it is to compare workers effective use of this time. Some aspects of recording make for easy comparison, for example, whether records are up to date. Others, e.g. the inclusion of essential data depending on worker's skill but also on client's motivation, present the supervisor with a more complex task.

The standard of social work performance is affected by the changing nature of the work, by its increased volume and new demands. This statement will not come as a surprise to social workers in social services departments where the effect of these phenomena is still being experienced. Hence standards can never be regarded as being even and fixed. The greater the new demands of the job the more variable the standard of performance. Standards are affected for the better by the provisions for sound staff development, by the quality of supervision and by the existence of an adequate support system. The existence of such facilities is likely to attract social work staff of quality, who in turn will make a positive contribution to the standard of social work practice in the agency.

The supervisor has an important part to play in the setting of standards. Initially she will rely on her own experiences as a supervisor in adhering to a standard, or, if new to supervision, use her own social work skill as a basis. Very soon however she will need to supplement her own experience by means of discussion and comparisons with other supervisors. In this way she will be able to acquire a wider picture of the range of social work performance within which a worker can be seen to be offering a competent service, an adequate service or a not good enough service to clients.

In this country, we now have the additional task of establishing how long it takes for a newly qualified social worker to build up enough expertise in relation to the broad service provided by the social services department. The widespread demands on social workers affect their pace and tempo in building up the kind of cumulative experience in one sphere or client group so essential to the development of social work skills. Previous expectations in relation to the speed by which expertise, e.g. in the child care field, could be expected to be developed are no longer relevant. The new structure in the social services department and the diversity of social work functions force us to consider anew the standards that can be achieved over a given period of time and especially the minimal standards beyond which practice must not be allowed to fall. This needs to be done in a systematic way.

Evaluation is a judgment based on evidence

In the absence of common standards it is especially important that any evaluative statement is backed by evidence (see Chapter 7). Feelings and hunches by themselves are not good enough. Evidence consists of observational or other relevant data that lends substance to what would otherwise be mere opinion. Inference without data is unconvincing. For example, it must be made explicit whether the statement 'excellent work with teenager' is based on many, a few, or just one case. Illustrations should be used to illuminate certain statements or to demonstrate the quality of work. An excerpt from a supervisor's evaluation on casework skills will serve as an illustration:

> In several of the cases she has discussed with me Mrs Robinson has demonstrated her ability to understand her clients and assess their emotional needs. However, there are cases where she has admitted to perceiving a problem other than that presented but has decided that unless the client asks her directly for help with this she should not take the matter up. An example of the way in which she limits her help with emotional problems is the assistance she gave to Mr C aged 68 – he is blind and lives with his wife, formerly a teacher. The worker recognized that this man not only needed the various practical aids to assist him adjust to his blindness but also that his loss of sight made him feel useless and ineffectual. She encouraged him to talk about his past and then suggested to him that he should write his autobiography. She was able to see that the autobiography came to an abrupt end at the point where Mr C lost his sight, which was quite sudden. He has written very little about his blindness or his feelings about it and the worker feels he has never fully come to terms with it. She knows that for some time he had hoped that a miracle would happen and that his sight would return but she has not been able to help him express his probable feelings of anger and/or disillusionment.
>
> In the case of Mr and Mrs F and Mrs N, the worker admits to having observed that they were experiencing some marital friction but she did not present them with any definite opportunity to discuss this with her. In fact, when the Fs did eventually come to her to ask for her help on this matter her immediate reaction was to attempt to

refer them elsewhere, to their GP, to marriage guidance, or to probation. With regard to Mrs N she had done nothing about the marital problem but had dealt with the family's financial difficulties. It was only when Mrs N eventually informed Mrs Robinson that she had been attending marriage guidance for some weeks that she discussed their marriage with Mr and Mrs N and since marriage guidance were now involved this was on a superficial level only. This difficulty in discussing emotional problems does to some extent affect Mrs Robinson's ability to formulate treatment plans and to evaluate the progress of some of her cases. I think she feels most at ease when dealing with practical problems and giving supportive help.

The supervisor has lent substance to her statement, that the worker limits her help to clients when she has to deal with emotional problems by relating her comments to three separate cases. While in the case of the blind man, it might be argued that the worker has made adequate efforts to help, this cannot be said of the work with the other two cases, when she took flight and avoided discussing what the clients themselves perceived to be a key problem.

Evaluation takes places within the framework of regular supervision and a well established professional relationship, and this makes it possible for evaluation to prove constructive, helpful and often stimulating. The purpose and the usefulness of evaluation should be discussed with the worker long before it occurs so that it can be seen as an essential aspect of supervision. Although evaluation is often feared and dreaded, those who have had the experience of careful and caring evaluation have found it to be a positive experience. Many workers under-value their qualities and skills, tending to see more of what is done badly rather than what is done well. An honest appraisal of the work can be reassuring and is unquestionably more welcome than a supervisor's silent acceptance or unspoken criticism that leaves the social worker perplexed and anxious as to how his work performance is being perceived.

Evaluation should be a shared task between worker and supervisor. Both are required to look back over a period of time and to take stock of the quality and quantity of work and to note this down in a systematic way. It is a task that will take time. Preparation has to be careful and thorough to be of use.

Towards a common minimal standard

Although we look at areas of knowledge and the degree of understanding of the worker, what is of significance is the way in which this understanding is being applied. Hence evaluation is eventually concerned with social work skills. What skills does a social worker require? How does he apply his knowledge about people to how they feel and function, for example, in situations of stress?

How many staff supervisors have considered in a systematic way the common criteria for social work performance? How many social service departments have actively encouraged their supervisors to pay attention to these important tasks and further, how many agencies have considered what is a common base for an evaluation of social work practice?

The development of common standards is desirable but the development of common minimal standards is essential. Without these, comparisons cannot be made, nor generalizations as to what can and cannot be expected of social work performance at any given level of professional development. Since the emergence of the all-purpose social worker, with opportunity for broad but shallow fieldwork experience, all supervisors experience difficulties in knowing what level of achievement can be reached at the completion of a social work course, and what quality of performance can be expected at the end of the first year of social work practice. In the absence of declared common criteria, and without the opportunity to compare findings, there is a danger that the supervisor's judgment may by weighted too subjectively, i.e. she may over-rate or underate certain skills based solely on her own experience and values. The existence, therefore, of an outside gauge that can adjust the balance is vital. Without some safeguards supervisors are justified in their reluctance to formulate judgements about the range and quality of social work performance.

There is a great need for supervisors to work together in groups to establish common criteria leading to the setting up of standards in social work practice. To this end three groups of supervisors have made a beginning in considering the skills required at certain phases of client contact:

Essential social work skills required at intake

GROUP 1	GROUP 2	GROUP 3
Establishing of climate	To listen, to observe and to explore	*To provide climate* Unhurried, uninterrupted confidence-giving discourse
Courtesy	Flexibility of communication	
Treating client with dignity	The capacity to hold the client's stress	Ability to listen and to hear
Appropriate bearing	The capacity to contain own stress	Ability to pick up communication (whether verbal or non-verbal)
Demonstrating ease of communicating	The ability to collect relevant information	
Empathic understanding		
Conveying a relaxed atmosphere		Ability to use appropriate language
		Ability to empathise
Containing anxiety (i.e. the client's, also worker's own)	*To provide a caring climate*	Ability to explore
	Acceptance	Ability to link
	Non-shockability	Ability to focus
Focusing attention on client	Empathy	Ability to select relevant information/observation
Exploration of situation	Self-awareness	Ability to use information to decide on appropriate action
Encouraging ventilation	To interpret agency policy and practice	
On occasions stopping flow of out-pouring		
	Linking up information towards the formulation of a diagnosis	Skill in limiting interview in relation to content and time
Towards establishing of a contract		
Eliciting client's expectations of agency help		Knowing when to say 'no' and skill in doing it
Declaring the setting of limits		
Clarity about direction		
Skill in recording		

The similarity of the selected criteria of the three groups shows that there is much common ground in social work thinking. The group contributions are shown in detail, and perhaps may prove an encouragement to supervisors to work out together in agency groups or elsewhere, common criteria for focused social work and evaluation.

Skill in initial contact, study, diagnosis, planning and treatment

1 Relationship with client
The establishing of initial contact requires knowledge, skills, and certain attitudes. All three groups have put emphasis on:

The establishing of a climate and stressed the attitudes and skills necessary to bring this about. What has not been listed so far are the environmental conditions required but often wanting in social services departments, a comfortable waiting room to enhance human dignity and a welcoming interviewing room in which unhurried, uninterrupted confidence-giving discourse can take place.

The ability to explore is a rare but an important tool. Asking pertinent questions and commenting in a way which stimulates further consideration are necessary skills which bring greater understanding of and by the client about his functioning, his motivation and his aim. The ability to explore stems from the social worker's understanding of unconscious factors and from a thorough knowledge of the subject matter. Unless the worker has specific knowledge of the problem area under discussion he will not know what questions to ask, and what leads to pursue in greater detail.

Empathy The ability to see, feel and comprehend to the full another's experience, even though the actual happening is outside the social worker's range of experience, is a major therapeutic tool.

R. Greenson (1960) in his illuminating paper makes the following comments:

> Most experienced analysts will agree that in order to carry out effective psychotherapy a knowledge of psychoanalytic theory and the intellectual understanding of a patient is not sufficient. In order to help, one has to know a patient differently – emotionally. One cannot truly grasp subtle and complicated feelings of people except by this "emotional knowing". It is "emotional knowing", the experiencing of another's feelings, that is meant by the term empathy. It is a very

special mode of perceiving. Particularly for therapy, the capacity for empathy is an essential pre-requisite ... Before proceeding further, I would like to attempt a preliminary definition of empathy as we use the term in psycho-analysis. To empathize means to share, to experience the feelings of another person. This sharing of feeling is temporary. One partakes of the quality and not the degree of the feelings, the kind and not the quantity. It is primarily a preconscious phenomenon. The main motive of empathy is to achieve an understanding of the patient.

The ability to develop and sustain relationships is essential at any stage of social work contact. The relationship is the vehicle for modifications of thinking, feeling and doing. Kadushin (1972) puts it in this way:

> The relationship is the communication bridge between people. Messages pass over the bridge with greater or lesser difficulty, depending on the nature of the emotional interaction between people. Social and emotional screens and barriers are lowered or become more permeable in the context of a good relationship. The readiness to return to the agency and the willingness to participate in the interviews are heightened. It is easier to be an open person in such a facilitative, benign emotional climate of mutuality and non-possessive warmth.

The ability to observe systematically is especially important during the period of study when facts have to be gathered, noted and assembled.

Observations on a mother's behaviour towards her child are quite as important as her own statements about her responses and contribute equally to the diagnostic picture. Observations of family interaction can often provide clues about the subtlety of a relationship that would take longer to obtain by other interviewing methods.

The ability to elicit client's expectation This skill can be seen as belonging to *the ability to explore*. It has been listed separately here in order to stress the importance. Consideration must then be given to the clients' expectations so that the nature of the contract is understood by the end of the diagnostic phase.

Essential social work skills required in Diagnosis (Assessment) and Planning

GROUP 1
Applying knowledge of emotional development and human interaction.
Linking + interpreting of material.
Assessment of client situation.
Assessment of need.
Assessment of ego strength or the capacity to use help.

GROUP 2
Selection of relevant information consisting of facts and feelings.
Noting of sequence of events.
Establishing client's strengths and weaknesses.
Recognition of relationship pattern and stage of emotional development.
Recognition of the motivation and capacity for self development.

Further skills required
Ability to stand back and think independently.
Capacity to withstand pressure and to plan rationally.

GROUP 3
Understand – assemble + assess
Select relevant information – facts, feelings – strengths, weaknesses.
Pinpoint problem areas as seen by social worker e.g. inability to face realities.
Ability to think independently.
Ability to work at client's pace.
Ability to take stock and see gaps.
Ability to say 'I don't know'.
Ability to resist pressures, internal and external.

GROUP 1	GROUP 2	GROUP 3
	Treatment plan	*Treatment plan*
	Establishing of client's needs.	Clarifying client's needs.
	Establishing of resources available including time.	Looking at all available resources.
	Ability to plan and to formulate.	Ability to plan short or extended work.
		Ability to sustain relationships.
		Ability to understand the nature of the relationships and the worker's part in it.
		Ability to discuss and to know when client(s) can make use of information/clarification.
		Versatility in relation to social work techniques.
		Skill in recording.

2 The overview

It is crucial to obtain as far as is possible at this still early stage, a comprehensive picture of the clients and their situation. This involves the gathering of all factors inherent in the situation, ordering these into areas of facts and feelings, strength and weaknesses; sorting out what belongs to the past and what to the present, what are individual and what are social factors. Skill in assembling ordering and selecting relevant data is of utmost importance.

The ability to take stock and see gaps is always an asset but especially at this stage. 'Assuming' and 'guessing' is misleading and relates more frequently to the social worker's difficulty in perceiving gaps than to the client's unwillingness to discuss further.

3 Planning

Good planning requires skill in setting realistic treatment objectives. This will take account of the worker's understanding of the client's needs, his knowledge of the available resources, and judgement as to whether the client will be motivated and has the capacity to use these resources.

Ability is required to stand back and think analytically coupled with the capacity to withstand pressures and plan rationally.

Treatment objectives require periodic reassessment and may have to be modified or abandoned altogether, either because of change in a client's circumstances, incorrect assessment of a client's capacity, or other factors that do not allow sufficient social work time for carrying through stated objectives.

Social workers need to guard against 'hanging on' to cases but should feel encouraged to ask questions about the feasibility of objectives.

4 Skill in offering differential treatment

This requires sound knowledge of human behaviour and motivation, understanding of social forces and a wide and varied repertoire of social work techniques. (Treatment techniques here include the whole range, practical service, environmental modification, support, clarification, insight giving, or any combination of these.)

The reader may by now begin to feel that not enough attention has been given to the emergency or crisis work that besets social services departments. There are many occasions when social workers are called upon to act swiftly and to take immediate action; often, but not always, that is what has to be done. The social worker's independent, critical thinking is essential when pressures to act are upon him from different quarters e.g. in the case of a possible emergency admission to a mental hospital pressures may come from the client's family or from a doctor. In cases of suspected infant battering neighbours or others in the community may press for action. On those occasions when it has been found necessary to take immediate action it is essential to do the thorough diagnostic thinking at a later stage – to postpone but *never* to abandon this vital process.

5 Skill in recording

That a large part of the social work profession has paid too much attention to *feeling* and *doing* and not enough to *thinking* is reflected in the general low level of recording. Most social work agencies demonstrate their lack of interest in this area by accepting erratic, formless recording from social workers.

Newly-qualified social workers offer no practical evidence that they have been taught in the methods of recording.

Nevertheless, most social workers would agree that recording is important although only a few demonstrate this by putting in sufficient effort, time and thought. Recording is still being treated as an unnecessary chore, an adjunct, rather than being recognized as the last essential step that concludes the interview. Until the worker has reviewed, assessed and recorded, the interview cannot be deemed to have been ended.

Poor recording is often indicative of poor social work practice although good practice is not necessarily reflected by good recording. There is however some connection between knowing what one is doing and adequate recording of what one has been doing. Skill in recording can only be as good and no better than the worker's perception, understanding and skill in interviewing. It is not possible to record what is not heard, seen or felt. A similar point can be made in relation to social work aims or objectives. If these have not been clearly defined and if the purpose of this particular interview is vague, the recording to follow will be similar in nature.

The content of a record is of the greatest importance while the style is of lesser account. The content is dependent on what the worker *sees* (that is, the quality of the observations), *hears* (the capacity to listen), *feels* (the quality of empathic understanding). What the worker perceives will largely depend on the extent of his knowledge in the problem subject matter. To take a simple example: in order to perceive that a child's development is retarded, careful observations must be matched by knowledge of common norms of child development. Without this knowledge the observations would be meaningless and would probably not even be made.

The knowledge the worker has at his disposal determines what can be perceived and seen, what can be heard and felt and what can be recorded. Inadequate knowledge relating to the client's problem results in poor social work practice which will be reflected in the record. The knowledge aspect is being stressed here since recording is frequently treated as if it were an isolated activity. Recognition needs to be given to recording as an integral aspect of the social work task; that the nature of recording is dependent in the first instance on the perception of the social worker which in turn is enlarged by the requisite knowledge. There are, however, other causes than inadequate knowledge that make for poor perception. The supervisor needs to keep these in mind when considering the social worker's records. Poor perception can result from:

1. inadequate knowledge in the subject matter of the problem
2. a worker's own uncertainty about his helping capacity which may cause him to cut short the client's account by e.g., uttering trite reassurances
3. over-identification with the client; that is the worker's own experiences, past or present, are getting entangled with those of the client, resulting in distorted perception
4. confusion as to objectives and uncertainty of focus.

Since recording is used for many different purposes, it is essential that in each instance, the primary purpose of the recording is made explicit. The purpose should guide the selection of content and style. This is an important supervisory task. One purpose for recording is the necessity to provide a documented account of services to clients and deals with the agency's accountability to the community. The need for this has become evident especially in cases of child battering when the agency tends to be seen as responsible for the death of a child. Allied to this is the need to record in such a manner as to ensure continuity at least between client and agency; the present day rapid turnover of social work staff makes this a particularly urgent consideration.

Social work records are tools for learning and for improving the service for clients. They help in respect of work already done by affording a chance to reflect and so possibly gain hindsight, and make it easier to plan work still to be done.

The social work objective within a given time, or the developmental stage of the case, should determine the content of recording. So, for example, during early client contact and until a diagnosis is formed it will consist primarily of information and observation relevant to assessment. One important area is the problem, and the record should therefore contain information as to how the client sees the problem, when it first occurred and under what circumstances; how long it has been in existence, and how the client has so far dealt with it; what has made it necessary to seek help now, who has helped her cope, how the client feels she can be helped by the social worker and agency. How does the social worker consider the client will use the offered help, does he recognize the client's feelings over seeking help etc.? Once the diagnosis or assessment has been made, subsequent material will centre on the helping process and its concomitants.

The level of the social worker's professional development should determine the mode of recording. Supervisors should insist that beginning social workers carry out process recording with at least a few cases. This is essential for the protection of the client and for the professional development of the worker. The beginning social worker is not likely to make a well selected and focussed record unless he has been given the opportunity to produce a detailed thoughtful one with evidence of reflective thinking. It is at a later stage that the experienced practitioner can be expected to record in a purposive, concise manner, selecting and organizing the relevant material with focus on the social work objective. But even the experienced worker will be well advised to use process recording on occasions especially when first-hand evidence is required to understand attitudes or feelings or when he cannot see the wood for the trees and is perplexed by the complexities in the case.

Essential in recording:

1 Note sufficient data related to the *purpose* of the objective, e.g. the nature of the problem and appropriate history, the client's view and feelings as verbalized and observed are required for diagnostic assessment.
2 State the social worker's comments on factors considered to be of significance in the interview(s).
3 Observe the client's use of the relationship and describe the interaction between client and worker. It is important also that the worker makes explicit his own contributions and responses, and declares their effect on the interview.
4 The social worker's deliberations should be contained in a diagnostic statement and subsequently in a treatment plan.
5 The movement (or lack of movement) in a case has to be made explicit. Summarised statements should be supported by observational evidence.

With practice, experience and good supervision, the worker will develop greater selection in what he does record. The clarity will then reflect competence rather than ignorance or omission which sometimes causes brevity of recording.

6 Assessment of attitudes as apparent through work

Principles of social work practice include acceptance of and respect for the individual. The social worker is expected to demonstrate this in his practice. There will be some, who, will not find this easy, who may pay lip-service to this principle but who in practice have difficulties in tolerating other people's different views and standards and who try to foist their own values onto others.

To change these attitudes requires self awareness on the social worker's part and a readiness to review, reconsider and modify. It also requires supervisory support and skill to further the development of self knowledge and control; the degree of self knowledge will in part determine the range of clients a worker can usefully work with; that is to what extent he can enter into the experiences of clients from different subcultures and understand those whose inner world is quite unlike his own. To acquire insights into personal preferences and to understand the effect of these on the work with clients is therefore all important.

Many workers are aware of their interest, their liking and identifications with certain clients, while others are not. Some workers recognize the tendency to reject certain types of clients, while others do not. This comment made by a social worker 'I love to work with deprived children but I try to control this interest' suggests a high degree of awareness. This is to be contrasted with another social worker who thought he had no hang-ups yet a close look at his caseload and subsequent discussion left one in no doubt that he worked actively only with those clients he liked. He however had no insight into this and was quite unaware of the effect of his attitudes on his total work commitments.

7 Criteria for the selection of clients and the management of the caseload

Because of complex and large caseloads workers must learn to manage these in a rational way.

The factors to be taken into account are:

1. people's urgent needs
2. their ability to take help
3. availability of help.

This presupposes skill in diagnosing needs, skill in assessing personality development i.e. ego strength, especially the client's motivation and his capacity to use the help in dealing with the problems, and his current and potential degree of insight.

4 knowledge about the *total* resources available:
   a) the worker's own resources
   b) agency resources
   c) other community resources.

It is important to see the total constellation and plan accordingly. The resources available (4) have to be related to people's urgent needs (1) and to their ability to take help (2).

Closely linked to this is the skill in limiting objectives, in being able to decide that a family cannot be helped in all the problem areas but can be helped in some.

A worker may have wide knowledge and skill in establishing a comprehensive diagnosis yet because he does not pay sufficient attention to the availability of resources, the client may end up by getting an erratic, unreliable service or virtually no service at all. It is more helpful to the client and gives more satisfaction to the worker if objectives can be related to existing resources and a realistic working plan is designed and agreed. It is not suggested that a social worker's knowledge of the shortage of resources gives him or the supervisor permission to gloss over clients' needs; whatever the circumstances, a comprehensive assessment is required with clients' needs made explicit. On occasions the shortage of resources has been used as an excuse for either an undisciplined way of operating or as a means of disguising lack of skill on diagnosing and planning.

What is required is a clear statement on client needs, the resources required, the resources available and those missing. Only in this way can gaps in the service be perceived by all who are responsible for a good service to all clients. Only social worker and supervisor are in a position to produce first-hand evidence of the 'not good enough service'. An honest declaration can be the first step leading to improvement.

8 Criteria for the management of a workload

This section includes the management of a caseload which forms a substantial part of any social worker's load.

Skilled timing is important. It requires judgment as to how long it will take to carry out certain tasks – be it interviewing, recording or some other tasks. Since experience plays a part, the experienced worker could be expected to perform better than the inexperienced worker. The worker's sensitivity and consideration for others, for clients and colleagues, also has to be taken into account. There are some social workers who are never on time to see their clients; there are others who are never on time for agency matters not directly concerned with clients.

9 *Skill in assessing the basis of pressures and ability to form an independent judgment and act accordingly.*
Social workers are exposed to many pressures during the course of their work, especially those in social services departments.
   Pressures can be:

1 External. These may come from members of the community e.g. councillors, headmasters, teachers, doctors, health visitors and others. These people have their own perception of needs and their own ideas as to how a particular client's problem should be dealt with and at times assert pressure to have a social worker act accordingly.
2 Client-pressure. The problems that clients bring to the social worker are of course of great urgency to the client. The social worker has to make his own judgement as to what extent this pressure is justified. He must not automatically succumb to one client, especially as it could be at the expense of another whose need is greater though he exerts but little pressure.
3 Internal departmental pressure. Social workers are frequently pressed in the direction of taking on an even larger caseload frequently resulting in a lowering of standards and leading eventually to ineffective practice. When the agency has no priority system, and when supervisors feel harrassed and troubled about the allocation of cases, it can at times appear easier for supervisors to push down on workers rather than up towards management. Allocation meetings, despite their apparent display of participation, can also put undue pressure on sensitive and uncertain social workers.
4 Internal personal pressure of the social worker. It is important to assess whether the worker's refusal to take on more arises from rational considerations and reflects strength even though it presents the supervisor with difficulties, or from other factors, like limited capacity or excessive anxieties and personal problems.

   Social workers want to help clients with their difficulties and are not easily given to writing people off. The task of telling some one in need that he cannot be helped is never easy and often is as unacceptable to the social worker as it is to the client. Yet, at times this has to be done, either because of lack of resources, or the client's inability to use what can be offered or because there just is no solution to some problems. This often produces feelings of guilt and anxiety for social workers and a tendency to deny the facts of this situation. Pressures too can be produced by anxiety arising from the nature of the work or certain aspects of it; newness and unfamiliarity of the job may cause the worker extreme anxiety and the load may feel very heavy indeed. It is therefore crucial that supervisors take appropriate steps to assess the real source of the pressures for the social worker.

Areas for evaluation

These areas for evaluation are meant as an encouragement to supervisors and workers to get off the ground a difficult but essential task that will facilitate better social work practice.

1   Knowledge of social provision in the following areas, and ability to use it appropriately
    a) The functions and resources of the department.
    b) The functions and resources of other agencies.
    c) Local community resources.
    d) Statutory requirements.

2   Social work skills
    a) To form and sustain good working relationships with clients.
    b) To understand client and assess his material social and emotional needs.
    c) To evaluate relationships with clients and to recognise clients and situations he finds easiest or most difficult to work with.
    d) To formulate realistic treatment plan (based on assessment of client's capacity and availability of social work time and/or environmental resources).
    e) To use constructively legislative power and statutory obligation when necessary.
    f) To evaluate progress of case.

3   Recording
    a) Keep up to-date records of events.
    b) Summarize progress of a case.
    c) Prepare appropriate reports.
    d) Write appropriate letters.
    e) Use recording as a tool for learning.

4   Management of workload
    a) Ability to assess priorities in planning work.
    b) Ability to make decisions on social work objectives that are related to the human, practical and financial resources available at that time in this particular social services department.
    c) Ability to handle emergencies and operate under pressure.
    d) Ability to allocate time for non-urgent work.

    e) Ability to estimate the time required for the carrying out of specific tasks.

5 Operation as a staff member
Within the department
    a) Availability for agency tasks
    b) Attendance and contribution at staff meetings.
    c) Attendance and contribution at team meetings.
    d) Relationship within the working group.
    e) Relationship with others in the organization.
Outside the department
    a) Cooperation with other social work agencies.
    b) Relationship with colleagues in other social work agencies.
    c) Liaison with significant people in the community.
    d) Relationship with significant people in the community.

6 Use of supervision
    a) For improving quality of work.
    b) For reviewing work.
    c) For planning work.

7 Assessment of achievement during period of supervision and future objectives.

9 Consultation

What is consultation?
There exists a good deal of confusion about the function of supervision versus the function of consultation. These terms are frequently used as if they were interchangeable; this is mainly due to lack of clarity regarding the aims and purposes of either. These are quite separate. There are occasions, however, when the term consultation is quite consciously used, or rather misused, because it is assumed that social workers will more readily accept consultation, and the use of this term is thus a conscious attempt to sugar the pill! Clarification of the concepts of supervision and consultation, their respective objectives, functions and boundaries, become therefore essential.

Consultation is one way of furthering the learning on the job. It is a process of interaction between two professional persons. The consultant (referred to as 'he') is a specialist in a particular sphere who makes available his expert knowledge and skill when the consultee ('she'), who herself has reached a reasonable level of professional development, asks for help in relation to a current work problem in an unfamiliar work area. The consultant's function is to provide opportunities for furthering understanding in relation to a *specific problem* or *subject area*. He may do this in a variety of ways; making available required information and knowledge; skilfully exploring alternative modes of operating, bringing to the fore knowledge and insights that already belong to the consultee; stating known facts or giving advice. A combination of these is not uncommon. The consultant will discuss alternative methods of collecting and utilizing essential data, and new ways of understanding and dealing with the many complexities in the client's situation. By the posing of relevant questions he will stimulate the consultee to re-examine ways of proceeding and thereby select a course of action most likely to lead to a satisfactory resolution of the problem. He may also offer assessment or diagnosis and actively advise on a course of action.

The consultant does not carry administrative accountability and therefore is not responsible for the implementation of the recommended action. The professional responsibility remains with the consultee; she asks for consultation in respect of a work problem when she feels the need for this but is free to accept or reject the advice and make of it what she will. This at any rate is the traditional pattern of consultation. The consultant, then, offers help in relation to a *specific limited area of work* and is not concerned with the consultee's total performance. His efforts are directed solely towards those areas of functioning that have been brought to him by the consultee who considers that in this instance she requires the consultant's expertise. The consultant aims at making this expertise available to the consultee for immediate use and for inclusion in the consultee's repertoire. Consultation can be asked for at any time. There is no regularity of pattern and the responsibility for action remains with the consultee.

Supervision has different objectives from consultation. The purpose of supervision is to ensure a good standard of service to all clients and the supervisor's responsibility is therefore related to the overall workload of the supervisee, ensuring as far as is possible that all clients on the caseload receive the help agreed by means of shared rational decisions. Supervision is a built-in and continuous process. The sessions are obligatory, they are planned and take place regularly. The supervisor is responsible for the quantity and quality of the supervisee's work, and on occasions may have to make decisions that are not in accordance with the current thinking of the worker. The supervisor is in a position to evaluate the worker's total work performance; this is never the consultant's task and would be outside his terms of reference. Since the social worker is accountable to the supervisor for his total work, the supervisor must be informed about his clients and must ascertain from time to time that the service is appropriate and effective and does not only exist on paper. To this end, supervision sessions need to be structured to allow time for enquiring into what might otherwise become the 'forgotten' or 'lost' cases, and also to find means to reassess in realistic terms what kind of service can be offered by this social worker to that client and to ensure its implementation. Because the supervisor carries accountability, she may have to use authority in a way the consultant cannot, and be prepared to exercise it in the interests of the client, though this may only be put to use on rare occasions. The supervisor has delegated organizational authority whereas the authority of the consultant derives solely from the recognition of his special competence and expertise.

The provision of special competence and expertise in the person of the consultant has been the traditional pattern of consultancy. This has been the case whether the consultant operated from within the organization or from outside. The latter practice usually occurs when the organization requires the known competence of a particular specialist who would otherwise not be available to the staff of the agency. For example, a number of family agencies and schools for maladjusted children have on their staff a consultant psychiatrist who, by arrangement, gives a certain number of hours to the staff. His main function is his special contribution in terms of knowledge and understanding of normal development and emotional disturbance. This he usually shares with the staff group as a whole but sometimes also with individual members of staff. Practices vary but are usually established with all concerned by agreeing on the pattern most suited to a particular organization.

The prime task is again to deepen the understanding of staff in respect to a particular problem area, by the systematic consideration of all the factors in order to arrive at a feasible plan of action that improves day-to-day contact and furthers healthy development.

In this country more recent patterns have included case work consultants in the health and welfare departments. These consultants had special knowledge, frequently in the field of mental health. Since the establishment of the social service departments, consultants in methods like case work or community work, have been employed in some departments, while in others consultants have been engaged to work with special problem areas, for example, fostering or delinquency. With the widened brief of the social services department, and the widespread functions of the social worker, consultants with specialist knowledge are gaining greater importance and are needed to improve the work capacity of the social worker and the service to clients.

Although the consultant's traditional role has been in a specific area where he is known to have a high degree of competence and expertise, recently organizations like the social services departments have used consultancy in somewhat different ways, i.e. in circumstances where it is not immediately apparent that the consultant has greater expertise than anyone else. For example, some consultants have been used to assist work groups in thinking through the implications of new structures, the composition of different kinds of teams, the functioning of team leaders, the organization of work allocation, etc. In many of these areas the consultant could not be presumed to have greater expertise in these new settings. In these circumstances his special contribution would be related to two main factors. He is an outsider; the situation under discussion is less personal to him and he is not directly affected by the outcome. He can therefore be presumed to be less involved and his thinking to be more objective. Secondly, consultants have as part of their equipment special skill in exploration and clarification; they have ability to elucidate participants' thinking and feeling. This is the precursor for constructive discussion, when alternative ways of operating and the consequences of certain actions can be weighted. This kind of consultancy can be carried out in group situations or with individuals. It can be undertaken by consultants who are staff members of the organization or by those from outside. In the latter case it is crucial that the consultant familiarizes himself with the pattern of the organization. He must know of the freedom and constraints within, have awareness of the work satisfactions and stresses, the mores and practices of organizational policies. Consultation, like supervision, does not take place in limbo and must be related to the framework of the organization.

Consultation is one way of helping people to learn more, both for social workers and supervisors and directors. Social work supervisors cannot be expected to have expertise in all the problem areas of the wide range of clientele. For this reason, consultation in relation to a particular area of work may frequently be asked for together by supervisor and worker; this is a rational way of proceeding and should be encouraged, especially as the supervisor (not the consultant) remains accountable for the work undertaken.

Frequently, when discussing the supervisor's support function to social workers, the question has been put, Who supports the supervisor? Supervisors need support whether by means of a support group or by having the use of a consultant. If either of these means is available supervisors will be more ready to support social workers, who will in turn offer greater support to their clients. Neither supervisor nor social worker can indefinitely function effectively without this. Support is needed in order to counteract the kind of depletion and draining that occurs in the social work profession when dealing continually with human unhappiness. In the absence of support, social worker and supervisor are likely to defend against the real understanding of human problems, ward off the pressures and anxieties in order to protect themselves in ways that lower the quality of the service to clients. It is extremely important that all supervisors, but especially those who are new to the job, have the support of a caring consultant with whom all aspects of supervision can be discussed and with whom personal insights can be shared. It may well be an advantage that the consultant, though intimately a part of the organization, is not in direct line management.

The professional worker should continue to learn all his life, but the means of learning should be different and in accordance with the stage of professional development he has reached. For example, supervision has as its aim to promote a high level of work competence. Consultation, on the other hand (when offered without the facility of supervision), takes for granted that there already exists a high level of competence and that for most of the time the worker can function independently. It is timely, therefore, to make a start in considering the criteria for work competence and, further, when the use of consultation may be the more appropriate vehicle for ongoing professional development. Some social services departments are now considering 'career grades' for social workers in order to ensure a better service to clients than is available at present. At the top end social workers will be needed who have a high degree of competence and expertise in one of the methods of social work or in one of the problem subject areas. In their own sphere, they should be expected to have a higher degree of competence than many supervisors. It would be reasonable, therefore, to assume that these competent practitioners will function with the aid of consultation rather than supervision. Consultation would seem to be the appropriate vehicle for ongoing professional development here. However, before this new practice can be put into effect, careful working out of criteria for work competence is required. Only very little attention has been given in the literature to this important area, hence a few criteria are offered here in the hope that the reader will add to and complement the criteria suggested.

1. The worker should have sufficient range of knowledge and skills to formulate differential diagnoses and to offer differential help or treatment to the majority of cases that are appropriately referred to the department.
2. The worker requires a wide-ranging repertoire of interviewing skills; quick and realistic perception of the client's mode of expression, so as to facilitate early and easy communication.
3. The worker should have sufficient self-awareness to know when consultation is needed. She should have enough motivation to ask for it and know how to use it. This presupposes the worker's understanding of her own strengths and weaknesses, of her knowledge and gaps, and that she has the confidence to declare her limitation. It is important that she maintains the ability to question her own performance and that she demonstrates readiness to use consultation when dealing with critical or unfamiliar areas.
4. The worker should have awareness of her own interests, likes, dislikes and prejudices and have acquired considerable control in these areas, yet be watchful and ready to seek consultation when she becomes puzzled by what seem irrational decisions or behaviour on her part.
5. The worker should be a responsible, participating member of the department and understand the aims and functions, her role and responsibilities as well as those of other staff members.
6. The worker should have up to date knowledge of the department's

resources both in terms of manpower and material resources and know how to use these. Beyond that she also needs to be aware of community resources and know how to make use of these for the benefit of clients.
7 The worker should be able to take responsibility for her total workload. This requires clarity in relation to objectives and ranking of priorities. It requires skill in organization, in timing and in the setting of limits.

The consultant's equipment

Consultation has to be built on the belief that learning is an ongoing process; he himself will be immersed in continuous learning. This fundamental belief is essential for giving sanction and for setting a model for the activity of learning. In the course of his functioning, the consultant will have to demonstrate his ability to listen, his quality of understanding and his skill in the differential use of the professional relationships. The consultant's equipment covers three separate but interrelated knowledge and skill areas:

1 Expertise in a particular area or subject matter
2 Consultancy skill
3 Teaching skill.

1 EXPERTISE

The consultant has to demonstrate that he has exceptional competence and specialist knowledge in a particular area or subject matter. This needs to be recognized by the organization and those who use him, but he too must be clear about his expertise and know that he has a special contribution to make. For example, a consultant in the area of social work supervision should be aware that he has the kind of theoretical knowledge and practice skills that can be transmitted to the consultees, linked for use to improve the quality of supervision. The consultant must not only be knowledgeable about his subject but be interested in it and in the learning of the consultees.

2 CONSULTANCY SKILL

The consultant should be clear about his contribution. He should gain satisfaction from enabling others to function that little bit better. He must be able to work towards long-range goals and find satisfaction in the slow and gradual process of helping others to achieve greater ease and competence in that particular aspect of their work. Like the supervisor, the consultant has to enjoy seeing others develop and become more independent. The consultant who cannot gain satisfaction from assisting others to do a better job, who is envious of the practitioner and would have preferred to go on practising himself, is unlikely to be truly helpful; he is more given to dwell on the consultee's weaknesses, feeling that he could do so much better himself. This attitude runs counter to the goal of consultation and to the role of the consultant. His role is always to enhance and strengthen the consultee's capacity and so to improve the service to clients. It is *never* the consultant's task to take away or to usurp the role of the consultee. This requires readiness and ability 'to teach how to do' rather than 'do'.

The consultant must be a sensitive diagnostician who is ready to put his knowledge and skill at the disposal of the consultee. A major task in consultation is to understand the consultee's problem and what factors have led her to seek help. He must ask if the consultee's difficulties in this area are due to lack of perception, incomplete understanding and skill. They may be due to poor planning or implementation or relate to an unusually complex task, or even to severe organizational limitations. The consultee's work difficulties and the particular timing for bringing these forward for consultation may also relate to personal problems or pressures aggravated or activated at this particular period. This can be a major cause for the consultee's own work skills to become ineffective. If this is seen as the difficulty, the consultant's task is a delicate one. He has to bear in mind the aims of consultation; to strengthen the worker's capacity to function more effectively in the area she has presented for consultation. He has to be clear that he is dealing with a consultee who is engaged in a work task and that his own contribution is in relation to the work problem. (This is a totally different situation from helping a client sort out his personal problems.) The consultant's function (while perceiving the personal problem of the consultee), is to strengthen or reinforce the consultee's capacity for reality-based perceptions and decisions, and to deal mainly in indirect ways (i.e. by means of discussing the client's difficulties in reality terms) with the problem that is the consultee's. However, it would be presumptuous to attempt to prescribe for the many complex situations that do occur. Suffice it to state that the consultant must be clear about the different role, responsibilities and tasks pertaining to consultancy as against those appropriate to social work practice. Further, he has to be watchful not to fall back on using methods from a former but different setting, particularly when he is new in the field of consultancy and is still more familiar with the methods and techniques used previously.

One of the essential skills of the consultant is to provide the climate that makes for ready discussion, exploration and reflection. Hence the relationship to be established is of major importance; it can either facilitate or hinder the process of consultation. When the relationship is secure, the climate is likely to be one where discussion can be free, where consideration of work tasks can be shared, where exploration can occur and hindsight be developed. Enabling communication affects both the climate and the relationship between consultant and consultee. The consultant needs to show adaptability. Though backed in his work by his own theoretical stance, the consultant cannot assume that the consultee has the same theoretical framework. This could be different altogether or less clearly defined than that of the consultant, even although the objectives may be similar. Hence a relaxed, open-minded attitude is required that enables the consultee to do her thinking without feeling constrained by a theoretical framework that may feel alien to her. The use of vocabulary must have meaning for the consultee. This again requires the consultant's quick appreciation of what any one consultee can use at any particular moment in time, and flexibility to act accordingly. This is especially important when a member of one discipline acts as consultant to a member of another discipline. In the past, psychiatrists and analysts have been the people most used in this way and have from time to time experienced difficulties in communicating helpfully with consultees. Increasingly, however, social workers are used as consultants in areas like residential work and have to be concerned to establish meaningful communications especially when the setting is not too familiar. The necessity to gain understanding of the organization in which the consultee operates is obvious and has already been elaborated.

The ability to perceive through the eyes of another person, that is, at second-hand, complex life situations or relationship patterns is an essential consultancy skill, but one that is not easy to acquire. It requires of the consultant the ability to draw out and explore with the consultee in such a way that the picture of the clients under discussion becomes more alive. Some consultees are very adept at this task, while others are not. This ability to perceive people or situations through the eyes of another is also the task of the supervisor. But the supervisor's task is easier in that she has regular ongoing contact with the supervisee whom she gets to know well and because of her knowledge of her total caseload can be expected to be more familiar with the supervisee's way of operating.

The consultant has to be prepared to be used as required by the consultee. He has otherwise no right of entry, even if he might suspect that consultation would be helpful. This requires ability to wait rather than to push in, and an inherent trust in the capacity and sense of others.

3   TEACHING SKILL

To exercise teaching skills the consultant must have knowledge of the essential factors of learning and teaching. He must understand how much the consultee knows about his specialist area, must take stock of her pattern of learning in order to consult in the most productive way, must appreciate the ambivalent element in learning and in consultation.

His teaching skills will enable him to establish the right balance between putting in and drawing out, as discussed in the chapter on 'Factors of Learning and Teaching'. Clarification follows on from exploration. The posing of appropriate questions in order to throw more light on the situation and to clarify possible alternatives, as well as understanding the consequences of alternative actions, is important. In order to do this well the consultant must be interested in the subject matter, interested in the consultee, and be able to hold together at the same time a number of different foci. For example, a consultant to supervisors must understand what is happening to the client, what the worker is trying to achieve, and how the supervisor is trying to help the worker towards this end. Although the consultant's main task is to help towards better practice of supervision, he cannot ignore the other two important people in this situation.

The consultant has to win credence before he will be given the opportunity to function effectively or even be used. This is particularly true of a newly-established hierarchial organization where many relationships have not yet been cemented due mainly to the newness of many roles and functions and the still too rapid turnover of professional staff. A new consultant can therefore be seen as a threat and has to work hard to establish trust and acceptance of his expertise. He has to be seen as having something to offer, as taking care to understand the dilemma of the worker, the nature of the work and the framework of the organization. Most of all he must win trust from those high up in the hierarchy who may not themselves have cause to consult him but who will bring influence to bear on those staff for whose benefit he has been appointed. Their influence will greatly affect his initial usefulness in the organization.

Finally, since consultation is now being used in so many different and diverse ways, it is important to get the contract clear within the total organization; the director, the line managers and the potential consultees need to be fully aware of its availability and use. Consultation, when properly used, has an impact on the total organization, and therefore everyone has a right to know from the start what its effect is likely to be. It is important for everyone to understand the nature of consultation and the way a particular organization has planned to implement it.

References

AUSTIN, L. (1952) *Basic Principles and Skills of Supervision in Social Work* Social Welfare Training Series ISTF/52/22

BELL, T. (1942) *Octavia Hill* Constable

BERNSTEIN, S. (1942) *The New York School of Social Work 1898–1941* Community Service Society of New York

BRODIE and AXELRAD *Mother-Infant Interaction Film Series* 'Resemblances in Expressive Behaviour' New York University Film Library

CAPLAN, G. (1959) *Concepts of Mental Health and Consultation* US Department of Health, Education and Welfare, Social Rehabilitation Service, Children's Bureau

CAPLAN, G. (1961) *An Approach to Community Mental Health* Tavistock Publications

CLEUGH, M.F. (1962) *Educating Older People* Tavistock Publications

DHSS (1968) The Report of the Committee on Local Authority and Allied Personal Social Services (Seebohm Report) HMSO

DEWEY, J. (1963) *Experience in Education* Collier Macmillan

GREENSON, R. (1960) 'Empathy and its vicissitudes' *International Journal of Psychoanalysis* Vol. XLI

HAMILTON, G. (1951) *Theory and Practice of Social Casework* Columbia University Press

HEINICKE, C. and WESTHEIMER, I. (1965) *Brief Separations* New York International University Press

KADUSHIN, A. (1972) *The Social Work Interview* Columbia University Press

MENZIES, I. (1960) 'The functioning of social systems as a defence against anxiety in the nursing service' *Human Relations* Vol. 13

PARKER, R. A. (1967) 'Social administration and scarcity: the problem of rationing' First appearance — former journal *Social Work (The English Quarterly)* April 1967

POPPER, K. (1972) *The Logic of Scientific Discovery* Hutchinson

REYNOLDS, B. (1942) *Learning and Teaching in the Practice of Social Work* New York: Rinehart
REYNOLDS, B. (1963) *An Uncharted Journey* Citadel Press
ROBINSON, V. (1936) *Supervision in Social Casework: A Problem in Professional Education* University of North Carolina Press
TITMUS, R. (1968) 'The welfare complex in a changing society' in *Commitment to Welfare* Allen and Unwin
TOWLE, C. (1954) *The Learner in Education for the Professions* University of Chicago Press
VICKERY, A. (1975) 'Specialist: Generic: What next?' *Social Work Today* Vol. 4 no. 9
WESTHEIMER, I. (1970) 'Changes in response of mother and child during periods of separation' *Social Work*
WHITEHEAD, A. N. (1962) *The Aims of Education and Other Essays* Benn
YOUNG, P. (1967) *Administration and Supervision of Staff in the Child Care Service* Association of Childcare Officers Monograph.

Bibliography

Austin, L. (1952) *Basic Principles and Skills of Supervision in Social Work* Social Welfare Training Series ISTF52/22
Austin, L. (1963) 'The changing role of the supervisor' H.J. Parad and R. Miller (eds): *Ego-oriented Casework* Family Service Association of America
Beard, R. (1970) *Teaching in Higher Education* Penguin
Bell, M. (1942) *Octavia Hill* Constable
Bernstein, S. et al (1942) *The New York School of Social Work 1898–1941* The Community Service Society of New York
Brodie and Axelrad *Mother Infant Interaction Film Series* 'Resemblances in Expressive Behaviour' New York University Film Library
Caplan, G. (1959) *Concepts of Mental Health and Consultation* US Department of Health, Education and Welfare, Social and Rehabilitation Service Children's Bureau
Caplan, G. (1961) *An Approach to Community Mental Health* Tavistock
Charity Organization Society (1897) *Content of Lectures Contained in Twenty-Eighth Annual Report* 1897 Charity Organization Society
Cleugh, M.F. (1962) *Educating Older People* Tavistock
DHSS (1968) *The Report of the Committee on Local Authority and Allied Personal Social Services* (Seebohm Report) HMSO
Dewey, J. (1963) *Experience and Education* Collier-Macmillan
Hamilton, G. (1951) *Theory and Practice of Social Casework* Columbia University Press
Hamilton, G. (1954) 'Self awareness in professional education' *Social Casework* Volume XXXV, Number 9
Greenson, R. (1960) 'Empathy and its vicissitudes' *International Journal of Psychoanalysis* Volume XLI
Heinicke, C. and Westheimer, I.J. (1966) *Brief Separations* Longman, International University Press, 1965, New York
Highet, G. (1950) *The Art of Teaching* New York: A Knopf
Judd, J., Kohn, R.E. and Schulman, G. (1962) 'Group supervision, a vehicle for professional development' *Social Work* Volume 7

Kadushin, A. (1972) *The Social Work Interview* Columbia University Press
Mattinson, J. (1975) *The Reflection Process in Casework Supervision* Institute of Marital Studies
Menzies, I. (1960) 'The functioning of social systems as a defence against anxiety in the nursing service' *Human Relations* Volume 13
Parker, R. (1967) 'Social administration and scarcity: the problem of rationing *Social Work* now *The English Quarterly*
Perlman, H. (1969) 'Teaching casework by discussion method' in Eileen Younghusband (ed) *Education for Social Work* Allen and Unwin
Pettes, D. (1967) *Supervision in Social Work: A Method of Student Training and Staff Development* Allen and Unwin
Popper, K. (1972) *The Logic of Scientific Discovery* Hutchinson
Reynolds, B. (1942) *Learning and Teaching in the Practice of Social Work* New York: Rinehart
Reynolds, B. (1963) *An Uncharted Journey* New York: The Citadel Press
Robinson, V. (1936) *Supervision in Social Casework: A Problem in Professional Education* The University of North Carolina Press
Robinson, V. (1949) *The Dynamics of Supervision under Functional Controls* University of Pennsylvania Press
Rycroft, C. (1970) *Anxiety and Neuroses* Penguin
Somers, M.L. (19) 'The small group in learning and teaching' in E. Younghusband (ed) *Education for Social Work* Allen and Unwin
Tash, M.J. (1967) *Supervision in Youth Work* National Council of Social Services
Titmus, R.M. (1968) *Commitment to Welfare* Allen and Unwin
Towle, C. (1954) *The Learner in Education for the Professions* University of Chicago Press
Towle, C. (1969) 'The place of help in supervision' in E. Younghusband (ed) *Education for Social Work* Allen and Unwin
Vickery, A. (1975) 'Specialist: generic: what next?' *Social Work Today* Volume 4, Number 9
Westheimer, I. (1954) 'Adjustment of overseas students in New York' *British Journal of Psychiatric Social Work* October
Westheimer, I. (1970) 'Changes in response of mother and child during separation' *Social Work Journal* Volume 27, Number 1
Woodcock, K. (1967) 'A study of beginning supervision' *British Journal of Psychiatric Social Work* Volume IX
Younghusband, E. (1969) (ed) 'The 'The teacher' in *Education for Social Work* Allen and Unwin

Index

adaptation stage 64–5
adolescent, delinquent 47–8
agency structure, familiarity with 33
assessment of social work functioning (*see* social work)
Association of Psychiatric Social Workers ix
attitude, to supervisor 25
attitude, to assessment 152
Austin, L. (1952) 15, 28
authority, use of 34–6

basic requirements 28, 40
'bedside manner' 28
Berkshire Social Services dept. vii, viii
blind persons' register 90, 91, 96
British Association of Social Workers ix
Brodie and Axelrad film series 50

capacity, of supervisors 27–8, 72–5
capacity to learn, and influence of culture 69–70
capacity, integrative 73
Caplan, G. (1959) 22
Caplan, G. (1961) 74
career structure 7
caseload management 78, 80–96
  supervisor's task in 81
  method of 81*ff*
  8-week plan 86–9
  and agency 90–6

casework process 39–41
Charity Organization Society (COS) 13, 14
children 2, 3, 10
Cleugh, M.F. (1962) 59
communication 5
concern, for clients 44
confidence, loss of 46, 48
consciousness of self 63–4
consultation, 27, 157–62
  different objective from supervision 158
  special competence 158–9
  in casework 159
  use in social service depts. 159–60
  equipment of consultant 162–5
  expertise 162
  skills in 162–4
  teaching skills in 164–5
court work, 85, 90
criteria: common 144
  selection of clients 152–3
  for management of workload 153–5
  for work competence 161–2
Curtis Report 55

delinquent, adolescent (*see* adolescent)
departmental structures, and supervisors 15–16
depersonalization 24
deterrents 3
development, of supervisor 36–7
Dewey, John (1963) 29

171

domineering parent 50–2

early learning climate 50–2
'educational diagnosis' (see social work functions)
emotional pressures 33–4
emotional states 74–5
empathy 22–3, 32, 58, 108, 144
enjoyment, in observing development 33
equipment 48, 49–50
evaluation 138ff
　nature of 138–40
　based on evidence 140–1
　areas for 155–6
expertise (see consultation)

French, Dr 73

'generic' concept 8
　definition 8–9
　service and caseload management 97
Greenson, R. (1960) 144
guidelines, for probationer supervisors 38

Hamilton, Gordon (1951) 8, 22
Hill, Octavia 13–14
Hodgets, Joan 90
Home Office Inspectors 85
housing stress 20–1

industrial action, effect on social workers 2
information on client 40
information, for social worker 61
insecurity symptoms 64

Joint Lectures Committee 14

Kadushin, A. (1972) 145
Kimball, Professor 18–19
knowledge: imparting of 28–9
　acquiring, 56, 73–4

Learning and Teaching in the Practice of Social Work 62
learning: ambivalence in 52–3
　climate for 57–61
　stages in 62–70
　rhythm of 70
　individual patterns 70–2
Lloyd-Owen, Dorothy 81
Local Authorities' Social Services reorganization 1, 2, 54, 139

management factors in supervision 16–17
management of caseload 41–2, 76
　(and see caseload; workload)
'manipulative' clients 31–2
Menzies, I. (1960) 22–3
motivation, of caseworker 22, 72–3

National Institute in Social Work Training vii, 103
National Union of Women Workers 14

objectives 77, 80
objectivity 21–4
office arrangements 16–17, 61
overload (see pressure of work)

Parker, R.A. (1967) 3, 4, 78
personality functions, in learning 53–7 (and see learning)
'philanthropy, school of applied' 14
planning 148
Popper, Karl (1972) 21
practice, of social worker 71–2

pressure of work   44–6, 55–6, 57, 74–5, 98, 99
pressures, on social workers   154–5
priorities, in caseload   41–2, 78, 79
Probation Officer   85, 91
projection   55

records and recording   149–51
regression   55
'relative mastery' stage   67–8
reorganization of social services (*see* Local Authorities)
Reynolds, Bertha (1942)   18–19, 57, 60, 62, 72
Richmond, Mary   14
Robinson, Virginia (1936)   138–9
Ruskin, John   7

Seebohm Committee   7
    emphasis on family aspect   7
Seebohm Report (1968)   2, 7, 55
    work range   9–10, 11, 27
shortage, of social workers   43–4
skills   39–40, 47, 58, 65
    essentials   143–4, 146–7
    in initial contact   144–5
    in differential treatment   148
    in recording, 149–51
    in assessing basis of pressures, 154–5
    in consultancy   162–4
    (*and see* capacity)
Smith, Susan   98
Social Inquiry Report (SIR)   85, 90
Social Services reorganization (*see* Local Authorities)
Social Work Today   8
social work: education   8–9
    functioning   106–11
    Model A – newly qualified worker, data report   112–3
    Model B – social work assistant   114–7
    'evidence'   110
    Model C – alternative approach to assessment   117–24
    Model D – unqualified worker   125–37
    performance standard   139–40
Socratic method   29
standard, common minimal   141–2
stress   74–5
    protection from   23–4
Stroud, John   4
supervision: initial aspects   14–15
    definition of support   19–21
    conditions for   26–7, 48
    objectives of   39–41
    (*and see* caseload; development; skills)
supervisory sessions   30–1
support: for social workers   4–5
    for supervisors   160
survival instinct   52–3

task and capacity   75–7 (*and see* capacity)
teaching: elements   17–19
    skills   30–2
    stage   68–9
    consultancy skill   164–5
    (*and see* skills; learning)
tier structure   6–7
time, organization of   42–3, 47
Titmus, R.A. (1968)   7, 10
Towle, Charlotte (1954)   58–9, 72
transference concept   31–2
travelling time   101

'understanding' stage   66–7

Vickery, A.   8

waiting list   3–4
Whitehead, A.N. (1962)   72
Women's University Settlement   14
workload: excessive   20–1
    in hospitals   23–4

management of 78ff
rationing of 78–9
three studies 98–105
competence criteria for 161–2

World Health Organization 22

Young, Priscilla 15